I0815183

WORD FOR WORD

RODNEY CROWELL

Eric Geadelmann

WORD FOR WORD

RODNEY CROWELL

Peaches

Now and then, Guy Clark would play his prized recordings of Dylan Thomas reading *A Child's Christmas in Wales* and *Under Milk Wood* and would reiterate his belief that the words to a well-written song should sound as good read aloud as they do when sung.

WORD FOR WORD

Art direction and design by Karen Cronin, Cronin Creative
Cover photo courtesy of Marty Stuart
All other photographs from the author's personal collection

Library of Congress Cataloging-in-Publication Data available upon request.

ISBN: 9781947026957

First printing

Published by BMG
bmg.com
rodneycrowell.com

CONTENTS

FOREWORD

You hold in your hands a treasure: selected lyrics from among the hundreds of wonderful, evocative songs that Rodney Crowell has written—each a little novella, describing a world with characters all its own. These songs are either the work of a great literary imagination, intimate self-reflection, or a crafty mixture of both. I know, for example, that Rodney Crowell didn't actually go to prison for seven long years but, on the other hand, he realizes, metaphorically speaking, the prison bars of his life's choices are no less solid steel. Those songs have led him to win just about every peer award for a songwriter there is, including Grammys, Americana Music Awards, Academy of Country Music honors, an ASCAP Founder's Award, and an induction into the Nashville Songwriters Hall of Fame. The awards aren't given specifically for the best melody, the most interesting chord progression, rhythm, or the best lyrics—*all* are essential to a memorable song. But my hunch is that the words were fresh on the voters' minds.

Stylistically, Rodney was embraced as part of the New Country movement along with Emmylou Harris, Lyle Lovett, Rosanne Cash, Steve Earle, and Carlene Carter. This was not a backlash against the Old Country of Johnny Cash, George Jones, and Tammy Wynette, but an appreciation and homage to them while injecting some new youthful energy and contemporary perspectives. It was in some respects similar to New Wave music, particularly by its leading craftsmen, The Cars, The Police, and Elvis Costello—all artists who had more in common with The Beatles, The Stones, and The Animals than with punk minimalists like The Clash, The Sex Pistols, and Social Distortion who were rebelling against the excesses of Progressive Rock. Like the New Wave artists, the New Country artists pushed at the boundaries of an old genre, avoiding its excesses and finding new meaning and expression while honoring its rich history.

Beginning in 1978, Rodney released five albums that put him squarely in the evolving world of mainstream country music, his landmark *Diamonds and Dirt* bringing him unparalleled success: five consecutive number 1 singles. And after that, four more Top 10s. By this time, he had already penned bona fide hits, huge hits, especially in cover versions by The Oak Ridge Boys, The Nitty Gritty Dirt Band, Crystal Gayle, Van Morrison, and Waylon Jennings—not to put too fine a point on it, but when a songwriter chooses to do another songwriter's song, it is about as high a compliment as you can imagine. Bob Seger's version of "Shame On The Moon" became *so* well-known, and so *associated* with Seger, that Rodney had to stop performing it for years because audience members thought he was doing a Bob Seger song. Same thing happened when Tim McGraw covered "Please Remember Me" and Keith Urban had a landmark hit with "Making Memories of Us."

Claudia Church

And then a funny thing happened on the way to the 2000s. Rodney decided he wasn't writing for anyone but himself. Museum pieces. His internal standard, his bar if you will, was higher than that of others—by now he knew what made for a good song, and he was not going to let himself be seduced by the promises of love, sex, and money that come from hits. Instead, he was going to do what any true artist does: keep trying over and over again to get it right, to write something that *he* could be proud of. We've become close friends over the years and privately he will admit that although there are some lines here and there, occasionally an entire song or two he feels good about, there's nothing in that wonderful repertoire that he would present to St. Peter, Moses, or Buddha and say "I am proud of this, it is the best I can do." There is a certain amount of internal torture that must go along with being him, a beautiful despair at listening to other great masters and feeling that he may never find in himself what he admires about their work. That instinct is what sustains all art and artists, the restlessness, the forever trying to improve. And if that's not the basic message of every major religion and school of theology, I don't know what is: the purpose of life is to try to become better.

I've never liked genre labels. What binds all his music together is that it is Rodney Music, unmistakably, even as he follows the twists and turns of a really interesting mountain road. Just as it's terribly misguided to classify Joni or Bob as folk singers or rock singers or what-have-you, great artists don't fit into a box because they are constantly trying to enlarge the box or make an entirely new one out of a material you didn't even know existed. Great songwriters show us what is possible with a song.

My own intellectual and emotional growth as a human being has been greatly shaped by the lyrics you now hold in your hands. If you spend time with them, they will grow to be cherished friends. They've moved me, comforted me, instructed me, and guided me. I came from a different tradition than Rodney. He was born in the big city of Houston in 1950; I was born seven years later in San Francisco but raised in a small town in Northern California. His parents had an emotional, rocky marriage; as he says: a house all topsy-turvy. I grew up in a house where logic was emphasized and emotion was something to be embarrassed about. We both turned to books and poetry and music to learn more about the world.

It is in the specificity of a good literary description that each of us is able to find our own connection. It is in the exquisite differences and details that we reach a common humanity. The experiences themselves may be different—the names, the faces, the particulars—but the emotions underneath them are what bind all of us together as writer and readers and listeners. We don't have to have been riding in the back seat of a '49 Ford the first time we heard Johnny Cash singing "I Walk Line," we could have been lying in bed late at night listening to a transistor radio, and still know the feeling of when those rockabilly rebels sent the devil running right through us. Rodney had a cane pole out the window; I had pear trees. Different details, same feeling, a feeling I had buried and didn't even have words for until Rodney reawakened them. And although Rodney's details aren't literally mine, they are emotionally mine. Now they can be yours, too. That's the power of a good song.

— Daniel Levitin, Los Angeles, California, July 2021

INSIDE A WOMAN'S HEART

MAN MUST KEEP HIS HEAD

cn open up the Doors

here ANGELS FEAR TO TREAD

~~A woman left lonely~~

~~Won't be that long~~

GO CRAZY

~~a~~ MAN ~~Move~~ ~~Freely~~

~~Wise~~ MAN ~~Move~~ ~~[illegible]~~ ~~Over~~

~~If you've Been INSIDE~~

you Been INSIDE Her

~~Once INSIDE A Woman's~~ HEART

(Don't Ever Let Her GO) How yo

TO

A MAN MUST Hold His ow

INTRODUCTION

There's a story my friend Susanna liked to tell about an Oklahoma City woman who, while visiting the Museo Reina Sofía in Madrid, noticed a smallish man daubing paint on the gallery's most famous painting. Frantically she cried out for a security guard to stop the desecration of the Guernica, to which the watchman casually replied, "That, señora, is Picasso, He works here." No doubt my friend's account, which is most likely untrue, is a variation on the famous Leonardo Da Vinci quote, "Art is never finished, only abandoned." That excerpt, I'm not ashamed to say, applies to some of the records I've made. As a songwriter, however, I'm far more comfortable with the Picasso yarn than the Da Vinci declaration. Revision is, for me, an open-ended part of the song-making process. Therefore, if you are at all familiar with the lyrics I've chosen to put forward in this retrospective, don't be surprised if some of my compositions have been modified to suit my ever-evolving sensibilities. As far as I know, none of the words are chiseled in stone. By the way, over the years I've heard a few songwriters say, "My songs are my children." To which I've been known to reply, "If my songs are my children, they need to get out of the house and find a job!"

— RC

Claudia Church

BACKSTORY

Even before my eighteen-month-old self first fixated on the exposed yellow lightbulb dangling from my parents' bedroom ceiling, the sound of my father singing had fully registered on me. Embedded in practically every early fragment of consciousness that I was somehow alive in a human body is the gauzy image of a young man hunched over a battered acoustic guitar with his eyes closed, pouring his heart into songs about frogs that went a-courtin', love letters written in the sand, and a little girl whose dying wish was for her mother to put her little shoes away.

Comparing these gentle performances over the first five years of my life to the raucous ones when my father made a no-guts-no-glory run at local honky-tonk stardom in the lowest of east Houston's low-rent establishments, I made no bones about my preference for his kitchen table repertoire. Though I knew he could ape the hit songs of the day better than every other Hank Williams wannabe in our neck of the southeast Texas woods, I couldn't help feeling that if the juked-up dancing fools were to hear his kitchen table rendition of "No One Will Ever Know the Truth But Me" they'd sit down, shut up, and pay closer attention to what this man was trying to say.

It wasn't due to lack of talent, or lack of trying, that only a handful of beer-joint patrons and jam-session friends ever realized just how good my dad was at interpreting the best of his generation's depression-era folk ballads and wartime country songs. While I was very much aware that something more burdensome than a common laborer's existence weighed heavily on his soul, it was decades before it dawned on me that, from my father's perspective, the stain of unfulfilled promise was all he had to show for his love of a good song. Whether he ever got over not being able to make a go of it as a performer, I can't honestly say. But I can happily attest that he wasn't the least bit shy about claiming the first few flurries of success that came my way as his very own.

As for my mother, what little attention she managed to attract in a family of nine share-crop farm kids was the result of her natural affinity for wordplay. Near rhymes and nonsense were her specialty, the more warped the better. "Mary had a little lamb, she tied him to the heater, every time he turned around he burned his little, middle finger." That sort of thing. But it wasn't until the sudden death of her first-born child that her flair for free-word association kicked into high gear. To cope with the grief of such a devastating loss, she became a fervent follower of charismatic, Pentecostal preachers in east Houston. By the time I entered the picture, she was so well known for her ability to speak in unknown tongues that she teamed up with one of them. Having witnessed their performances

countless times, I can offer a composite account of their collaboration. Three quarters of the way through the reverend's fiery sermon, she'd let go with a staccato volley of hard consonants, soppy vowels, high pitched squeals, and guttural moans, the combined meaning of which her partner made a big show of decoding for his spellbound congregation as "messages from God on high." Looking back, the whole thing seems rehearsed. And by the second or third of fifty or so re-enactments, it most certainly was. Nevertheless, I believe my mother's role in these shenanigans came straight from the heart. As for the minister, I'm not so sure.

THE ROLLING TONES

SELECTED LYRICS
PART ONE

May your nights be filled with more
And your days with honest work
May you wake up smelling roses
When your face down in the dirt
May the answers to your questions
Fall like raindrops on your head
May you find your place in Heaven
Fore the Devil knows your dead

Ooh set em up drink

Gin 'n' pocket knife

May you always stay in touch
With the things that keep you young
When you're staring at injustice
May you never bite your tongue
May your tender years past seventy
And your sunsets take their time
Here's to happy ever after though you
Haven't got a dime

Ooh here's to love here's to life
From the fair and tender milk maid
to the old crazy farmer's wife

Ooh set em up drink em dry
We may never live forever
But we shure as hell can try

We may not live forever
But we shure as hell can try

The Flyboy and the Kid

May the wind be at your back and the world sit at your feet
May you waltz across Wyoming with a rose clutched in your teeth
May the answers to your questions fall like raindrops right on cue
May you set up shop in heaven before the devil knows you're due

Ooh, here's to love, here's to life
All the fair and tender ladies and the plain dirt farmer's wife
Yeah, here's to you, here's to me
Some ole mad dog mountain flyboy and the kid from Tennessee

May your nights be filled with laughter and your days with honest work
May you wake up smelling roses when you're face down in the dirt
If you had the sense to come in when the storm clouds start to grow
You wouldn't be my right hand and the best friend that I know

Ooh, here's to life, here's to love
When your heart beats like a lion's and your shoes fit like a glove
Yeah, here's to you, here's to me
Some ole mad dog mountain flyboy and the kid from Tennessee

May you always stay in touch with the things that keep you young
And when you're staring at injustice may you never bite your tongue
May the bear tracks in your future find you downwind in a glade
Where the grass as green as absinthe comes in forty different shades

Ooh, here's to love, here's to life
All the fair and tender ladies and the old fish-monger's wife
Yeah, here's to you, here's to me
Some ole mad dog mountain flyboy and the kid from Tennessee

Yeah set 'em up, drinks for free
It's the mad dog mountain flyboy
And the kid from Tennessee

How much love can one man take
How far must I bend before I break
Seasons change but you remain the same
How

The hour is early the whole world is quiet
Another tomorrow about to ignite
I'm ready for danger ready for fire
Ready for angels to lift my soul higher
Life's been good to me
I'm pretty where I want to be
The grass is green here on this side
I've got a past I want soon forget
But you ain't [illegible] nothing yet
I'm just [illegible] how to fly
I tried goin faster tried slowing down
Tried to get past every heartache in town
A dream can die here with old hearts to break
Can't let down your guard when there's so much at stake

A new day is forming not far down the road
The first shades of morning are about to explode
I'm halfway to heaven halfway to hell
I might roll a seven you never can tell

This Life I'm Living IS the Best I've Got
Thats why I want to Give It my Best Shot

Lifes Been Good I Guess
my Racket of Hearts Been Blessed
with So much more than meets the Eye
I've Got A Past Full of Sticks & Stones
& A Good helm in my Bones
I'm Just Learning How to Fly

Its the Dreams that are Hard with old Hearts to Break
you Can't Let Down your Guard when theres So much at Stake
when your Halfway to Heaven Half way to Hell
you might Roll A Seven you never can tell

Lifes Been Good I've Said I Can't Quit while I'm Ahead
I'm 10,000 miles A Head
The Day I Rest Is the Day I Die
I've Got A Past

I want to Go Faster I Dont want to Slow Down
I Dont want to Give up on this merry Go Round
A new Day Is Forming Its not Far Down the Road
the First Stems of morning Are About to Explode

Still Learning How to Fly

The hour is early, the whole world is quiet
A beautiful morning is about to ignite
I'm ready for danger, I'm ready for fire
I'm ready for something to lift me up higher

Life's been good, I guess, my ragged old heart's been blessed
With so much more than meets the eye
I've got a past I won't soon forget, you ain't seen nothing yet
        I'm still learning how to fly

It's the dreams that die hard with old habits to break
You can't let down your guard when there's so much at stake
I'm halfway to heaven, halfway to hell
But I might roll a seven you never can tell

Life's been good, it's true, when I'm feeling just like new
The same old rules need not apply
I've got a past full of sticks and stones, and a good feeling in my bones
        I'm still learning how to fly

I want to go faster, I don't want to slow down
I don't want to get off this merry-go-round
I want to be reckless, I want to be vain
I want to make love like a runaway train

"Life's been good," I've said, I'm ten thousand miles ahead
The day I rest is the day I die
I've got a past like a broken wing but you ain't seen anything
        I'm still learning how to fly

        (for Ernest Chapman)

Jewel of the South

One fine morning when the wild geese fly
I'm taking my chances on the sunny side
I'm headed down south where the grass grows tall
Where the mocking bird's singing and the whippoorwill call
Spanish moss on the Natchez Trace, Gulf wind blowing wide across my face
French girls dancing to a big bang drum back down south where I come from
Where the river flows like warm molasses, rain fogs up my reading glasses
Honeysuckle strong enough to curl your hair . . . back down there
Jewel of the South, cross my heart, shut my mouth
Come the morning I'll be home in the sweet Delta dawn

One fine morning, gonna pull up stakes, gonna chalk it all up as a bad mistake
Hit the decks running, bid a fond farewell
By the time I get to Memphis I'll be out of my shell
Cotton fields just as white as snow, sweet magnolia blossoms grow
Big moon shining like an ice cream cone back down south where I belong
Where the river flows like milk and honey
The nights are slow and the eggs are runny
I wouldn't mind sitting in a rocking chair . . . back down there
Jewel of the South, cross my heart, shut my mouth
Come the morning I'll be home in the sweet Delta dawn

One fine morning, and it won't be long, I'm leaving out early with my glad rags on
I'm gonna pull a load of wool off my own two eyes
And sharpen my senses counting railroad ties
When the mile-long trestle makes a clickity-clack
The whole damn town is gonna welcome me back
I've got a ticket to the land of sugarcane back down on the Pontchartrain
Where the river flows like Grand Marnier, sweet olive takes my breath away
Sunday morning walk along the Jackson Square . . . back down there
Jewel of the South, cross my heart, shut my mouth
Come the morning I'll be home in the sweet Delta dawn

One fine mornin 'bout the break of day
I'm leavin out early got to get away
talkin way down south

I'm gonna hit the deck runnin say some short goodbye
By the time I hit Memphis I'll be 20 feet high

when the wild geese fly

One fine mornin gonna pull up stakes
When it hurricane season
Gonna part my hair on the other side

One fine morning
Gonna stand up tall
Hurrican season
Leave a wake up call
Sharpen my senses
Lighten my load

Spanish moss grows thick along the Natchez Trace
Gulf wind blowin cross my baby's face
lightly free

French girls dance & sing the whole night ~~away~~ long
Barefooted all night long
~~to~~ their own sweet song
Thats where I belong

Look right down the ~~throat~~ horses mouth
At the jewel of the south
I'm talkin way down south

Cotton fields white as snow
Sweet magnolia blossom grow
Full moon lookin like an ice cream cone
Back down south where I belong
One fine morning when the wild geese flyin

When its hurricane season some fine day when the

Jewel of the south
Cross my heart
Shut my mouth
In the mornin
I'll be home
In the sweet
Delta dawn

shut my mouth
~~Way~~ down south where the grass is green
Where the sky is blue & the red birds sing

Landscape lays beneath
ol' man
Lazy River flows like Father Time
Rail road trestle
Crazull vines
Hurrican season leaves a wake up call
St Charles Avenue
street car lines
Audobon Park
Dry September & ~~the Hurricane~~

Ol man River flows like warm molasses flows
Summer rain fogs up my reading glasses slow
Honey suckle assaults my senses
my defenses

Dry September
& the Hurricane
Blow

ns

Sharpen my Senses Walk & Lighten my Load
Point my Buggy Down a Red Dirt Road
Old Man River Flows Like warm molasses Flow
Honeysuckle Vines Distort All my sense of time
~~Summer Rain So~~ Soft
Dry September Calls Far beyond these City Walls
Wild Birds Fly By Night Wild
Land of Sugar Cane Along the Ponchatrain

Jackson Square
Rockin Chair

River Flows Like Milk & Honey

Gonna Sharpen my senses on a Southern Drawl

Im Gonna Roll the wool off of my own Eyes
Sharpen my Senses
Counting RailRoad ties

Day -
One Fine Morning when the Wild Geese Fly
Gonna Part my Hair on the Other Side
Gonna Head Down South Where the Grass is Green
where the Sky is Blue & the Red Bird Sings
Spanish Moss on the Natchez Trace
Gulf Breeze Blowin Cross my Face
French Girls Dance & Sing the Whole Night Long
Back Down South Where I Belong
River Flows Like warm molasses
Rain Fogs up my Reading Glasses
Honeysuckle whispers on the Midnight Air
Summer Night Air
my Senses walks on Air
my Best Defenses
Back Down There
Swinging on a Cudzuh Vine

Crully Weather

Sugar Hair Sparkle on a Wild March Hare

Love the Land of Sugar Cane
Back Down on the Ponchatrain

morn
One Fine Day Gone Pull up Stakes
Chalk it up As a Bad Mistake
RailRoad Trestle & the Cudzuh Vines
Audubon Park & the Street Car Lines

Gonna Point my Buggy toward the Promised Land
Gonna Get Back Down There
Just As Quick As I Can

It Ain't Over Yet

It's like I'm sitting at a bus stop waiting for a train
Exactly how I get here is hard to explain
My heart's in the right place, what's left of it I guess
But my heart ain't the problem, it's my mind that's a total mess
With these rickety old legs and these watery eyes
It's hard to believe that I could pass for anybody's prize
Here's what I know about the gifts that God gave
Ah, you can't take them with you when you go to the grave

It ain't over yet, ask someone who ought to know
Not so very long ago we were both hung out to dry
It ain't over yet, you can mark my word
I don't care what you think you heard
We're still learning how to fly
It ain't over yet

For fools like me who were built for the chase
It takes the right kind of woman to help you put it all in place
It only happened once in my life but, man, you should've seen
Her hair two shades of fox-tail red, her eyes some far out sea blue green
I got caught up making a name for myself, you know what that's about
One day your ship comes rolling in, the next day it rolls right back out
You can't take for granted none of this shit
The higher up you fly, boys, the harder it is you're gonna get hit

It ain't over yet, I'll say this about that
You can get up off the mat or you can lay there till you die
It aint over yet, here's the truth my friend
You can't pack it in and we both know why
It ain't over yet

Silly boys blind to get there first
Think of second chances as some kind of curse
I've known you forever and ever, it's true

If you came by it easy you wouldn't be you
Make me laugh, you make me cry, you make me forget myself

Back when down on my luck kept me up for days
You were there with the right words to help me crawl out of the maze
When I'd almost convinced myself I was hipper than thou
You stepped up with a warning shot, fired sweet and low across the bow
No, you don't walk on water and your sarcasm stings
But the way you move through this old world sure makes a case for angel wings
I was halfway to the bottom when you threw me that line
I'll quote you now verbatim, "Get your head out of your own behind"

It ain't over yet, what you wanna bet
One more cigarette ain't gonna send you to the grave
It ain't over yet, I've seen your new girlfriend
Thinks you're the living end, great big ole sparkle in her eye
It ain't over yet

(for Guy)

I'd ask how I got here but I couldn't care le[ss]
It's the sins of a lifetime that's causing me stress
I wish I could tell you how I got in this mess
It's like I'm sittin' at a bus stop
waitin' for a train
Just how I got here is hard to explain
My heart's in the right place
What's left of it I guess
But my heart isn't the problem
It's my mind that's a mess
These rickety old legs badly couldn't care less
It's these rickety old legs + these watery eyes
+ a straw head of hair that a young man dyes

& forget how I got here
with my hea[d in] the clouds
Like an ol[d] weather vane
As rusted + pointless as an old weather vane

Earthbound

I could shed my skin and in the blink of an eye I could fly, fly, fly
Tie my dreams up in a sack, lay my head down on the track and die, die, die
My life's been so sweet I just can't stand it, I must admit I've made out like a bandit
Last night's conversation with a real good friend of mine, drinkin' wine, wine, wine
Said fifty years of living and your worst mistakes forgiven just takes time, time, time
One man's lust for life brings world renown
The next guy can't get two feet off the ground . . . earthbound

Earthbound, hear the wind through the tops of the trees
Earthbound, summer sun nearly ninety degrees
Earthbound, big old moon sinkin' down
Think I might stick around . . . I'm earthbound

I knew love once way back when, she had almond eyes and olive skin
And long black hair
She was Irish/Spanish mix-breed, I was southeast Texas hayseed
We were almost there
Her daddy did not like my kind around, and true love took the next train out of town . . . earthbound

Earthbound, where there's fathers and daughters in pain
Earthbound, mama's boy walkin' home in the rain
Like a ship run aground
Think I might stick around . . . I'm earthbound

With each new day that passes I'm in need of thicker glasses but it's all okay
Someday I'll be leaving but I just can't help believing that it's not today
Every golden moment I have found, I've done my best to run right in the ground . . . earthbound

Earthbound, winter sky big and beautiful blue
Earthbound, fallen angels come calling on you
Earthbound, keeping close to the ground
Think I might stick around

Earthbound, Tom Waits, Aretha Franklin, Mary Karr
Earthbound, Walter Cronkite, Seamus Heaney, Ringo Starr
The Dali Lama and Charlie Brown make me want to stick around . . . I'm earthbound

(for Steuart)

earthbound...
...bodhisattva chooses ... someone has to show the
way... and turn out the... lights... and make sure...
no... one... gets lost... in the illusion... reality hurts...
but it's better...

East Houston Blues

So, I grew up hungry and I grew up hard
Took the streets and alleys for my own back yard
I've got a "break and enter" on my list of crimes
Been before the judge one too many times

East Houston blues, scale of one to ten
About a nine-and-a-half is where it's always been
It's in the drinking water and in the bar ditch mud
East Houston blues gets in a poor boy's blood

I learned to drink and drive when I was twelve years old
My Uncle Fireball Stoddard, rest his ragged soul
He ran a fifty-four Ford up and down the drag
Sipping Early Times straight from a paper bag

East Houston blues, picture Dowling Street
And Navigation Boulevard where the crossroads meet
Three sheets in the wind, brick shy of a load
East Houston blues down a nowhere road

Forty-dollar boots, big bangora hat, stolen money from an inside job
Maybe think about that

I'm a third ward child, my mother's only son
Which means exactly nothing without a loaded gun
I don't believe in love, this I guarantee
If there's a God above, he's got it in for me

East Houston blues, what you want me to say?
I need to find me a woman, keep the wolves at bay
Keep my head on straight, maybe toe the line
East Houston blues ain't no friend of mine

Just so you understand that of which I speak
I'm a worried man on a losing streak

Hank DeVito

Lightning Strikes Quite Likely where you stand — where you stop
In the shadow of the Astrodome the kids are right at home
Swimming in the streets to beat the band
Skiing in a bar ditch behind a moped
Slice my self wide open on a sardine can
Summertime is here the only thing to fear
Is the rain will come the coming of the ice cream man
Just a dirt poor Houston kid with his family on the skids
But I always had a nickle for the ice cream man

Mosquito truck blows clouds of DDT
Air raid buzzer wailing way up high
Me + Dabo Buck used to run behind that truck
Pretending bombs were falling from the sky

Telephone Road

It was one of those
Kind of places

Them Rockabilly Re
Runnin Reckless

Split a pine in half

You could tell when they
were feeling Happy

Telephone Road

Rain came down in endless sheets of thunder
Lightnin' bolts split pine trees down to the roots
In the shadow of the Astrodome with a hurricane coming on strong
We used to hit the streets and go swimmin' in our birthday suits

Skiing in a bar ditch behind a moped
Thirteen stitches on the corner of a sardine can
We were dirt poor Houston kids, our whole family living on the skids
But we always had a nickel for the coming of the ice cream man

Mosquito truck blowin' up DDT, barefoot heathens runnin' wild and free
Air raid buzzer at a noon day scream, living in a dream on Telephone Road

I used to love them cherry Cokes down at the Prince's drive in
And the cheeseburgers taste so good I like to come untied
There's a chinaberry tree I remember I used to climb in and out of my window
The night I left was on the day before my grandma died

Sawdust spread out on a dance hall floor, juke box rippin' up an all-out roar
Bar maid smilin' at a ten-cent tip, livin' is a trip on Telephone Road

> Magnolia Garden bandstand on the very front row
> Johnny Cash, Carl Perkins and the Killer puttin' on a show
> I was six years old and just barely off my daddy's knee
> When those rockabilly rebels sent the devil runnin' right through me

Drive-in movie in the trunk of my car, one-eyed sailor in an ice house bar
Spit-shine Charlie and peg-legged Bill all dressed up fit to kill on Telephone Road
Bar-b-que and beer on ice, a salty watermelon slice
Down at the Little Taste of Paradise on Telephone Road

The Rock of My Soul

The rock of my soul went to church on Sunday
The rock of my soul went to work on Monday
Clean across the levee by the railroad track
The other side of Houston in a two-room shack
Sweeping out confetti from a third-grade classroom
The rock of my soul pushed a dust mop broom

The rock of my soul didn't have much luck
He came to town grinning on a flat-bed truck
The rock of my soul didn't have much charm
With the lack of education on a red dirt farm
He was fond of disappearing on an eight-day drunk
Coming home smelling like a lowdown skunk

And he said, "Do like I say, and not like I do, and you might make me proud"
Another Houston kid on a downhill skid for crying out loud

I'm a first-hand witness to an age-old crime
A man who hits a woman isn't worth a dime
5-6-7-8-9 years old, that's what I remember 'bout the rock of my soul
I told him I would kill him if he did not stop it
But the rock of my soul just would not drop it

I learned to lie like dirt, I could steal your shirt and talk with a gun
Another Houston kid on a downhill skid, like father like son

I got out of prison about a year ago
Seven long years really went by slow
I didn't kill my daddy but my mama tried
She shot him with a pistol and he like to have died
I'm on probation living straight and true
And there is every indication that they are too
That's all I know about the rock of my soul

Oo oo oo

Rock of My Soul ?

He said do like I say not like i do
You might make me proud
We're just white trash son
On a down hill run
For crying out loud

What it was back then you've gotta understand
The fire in the clouds
You learned to lie + cheat
+ never miss a beat
For crying out loud

You wanna roll the dice
You gotta pay the price

He could lie like dirt
He could steal the shirt
Right off your back
He was wired on speed
He was hard to read
+ sharp as a tack

I learned to lie like dirt
Steal your shirt
+ talk with a gun
In the white trash rules
you learn to suffer fools
cause thats how its done

Another hopped up kid
on a down hill skid

Steal without thought

Just a hopped up kid
on a down hill skid

I learned to lie like dirt
Steal your shirt
+ talk with a gun
Before I was ten
I was raised on shame
Its a small time game

White trash trait

I learned to lie like dirt + I could steal your shirt
Before I could talk
Playin white trash rules you learned to suffer fools
Before I could walk

I Wish It Would Rain

Turning tricks on Sunset, twenty bucks a pop
Some out-of-town old businessman or an undercover cop
I'm living with the virus flowing way down in my veins
Oh, oh I wish it would rain

I know you've heard my story or seen me on the street
Just another cracker gigolo dressed up like trick-or-treat
Now you may want to judge me or treat me with disdain
Oh, oh I wish it would rain

Memphis, Texas, Houston, Tennessee
I'm just so turned around I don't know where I want to be
This California desert is driving me insane
Oh, oh I wish it would rain

So, I squandered my resistance taking any kind of drug
I'd smoke or shoot or eat it, I'd drink it from a jug
And I offer no excuses for your sympathies to gain
Oh, oh I wish it would rain

Everybody knows me as the kid
I've made it seven years still I don't know how I did
I come from a long line of live and love in vain
Oh, oh I wish it would rain

So, I pray to Mother Mary, I've even seen a priest
When the angels come to get me, I know I'll be released
I'll leave this mean ole desert bound for Memphis on that train
Oh, oh I wish it would rain
Oh, oh I wish it would rain

Wandering Boy

Come in from the cold, you must be cold
Threadbare against a freezing wind is a short time getting old
Come and sit down, tell me where you've been
Rest your soul beside the fire till it's time to go again

Take me back one more time
To where the railroad track meets the kudzu vine
Wandering boy

The blood that's flowing through you flows through me
When I look in any mirror it's your face that I see
You're my only brother, I'm your twin
And you've come home to rest a while and shed your dying skin

Ease your mind, have no fear
When it comes your time, I'll be here
Wandering boy

We're two Houston kids sailing mason jar lids with our pop bottles hid
By the bayou's bend in the wild east end, welcome back again
Wandering boy

I used to cast my judgements like a net
All those California gay boys deserve just what they get
Little did I know there'd come a day when my words would come back screaming
Like a debt I have to pay
Lean on me, I'll be strong, you're almost free, it won't be long
Wandering boy

We were two Houston Kids
Sailin Mason Jar Lids
Out on Pop Bottle Road
Catchin Katydids
In the Bayou Bend
In the Wild East End

We were two Houston Kids
Sailin Mason Jar Lid
with our Pop Bottles Hid
Where the Bayou Bend
& the Sidewalk End
& were Back Again

I Walk The Line Revisited

I'm back on board that '49 Ford in 1956
Long before the sun came up, way out in the sticks
The headlights showed a two-rut road way back up in the pines
The first time I heard Johnny Cash sing "I Walk the Line"

I got my thrill behind the wheel upon my daddy's lap
Grandpa rode co-pilot with a flashlight and a map
Cane pole out the window, it was in the summertime
First time I heard Johnny Cash sing "I Walk the Line"
  I keep a close watch on this heart of mine
  I keep my eyes wide open all the time
  I keep the ends out for the ties that bind
  Because you're mine, I walk the line

I never will forget that day, I know the time and place
It sounded like the whole thing came right down from outer space
I still can see those headlights and the dashboard in my mind
First time I heard Johnny Cash sing "I Walk the Line"
  I find it very, very easy to be true
  I find myself alone when each day's through
  Yes, I'll admit that I'm a fool for you
  Because you're mine, I walk the line

All these long years later, it's still music to my ears
I swear it sounds as good right now as anything I hear
I've seen the Mona Lisa, I've heard Shakespeare read real fine
It's just like hearing Johnny Cash sing "I Walk the Line"
  As sure as night is dark and day is light
  I keep you on my mind both day and night
  And happiness I've known proves that it's right
  Because you're mine, I walk the line
  Because you're mine, I walk the line

RC & Johnny Cash, 1996

Put away 15 grand doing one night stands
Mostly liquor stores and filling stations
Me + a peeping Tom by the name of J.D. Swan
+ any number of his odd blood relations

It was armed robbery 1957 mostly our getaways were clean
In ky of the boys and bury the bread
out off of Highway 17

I had 5 kids a wife with one dress
+ a yard full of cars that went run
my two oldest boys were on to my noise
and they despised what their daddy done
I did what I did the best I could
making my plans by the light of day
then the night would fall + it was time to call
+ I was always on my way

FROM THE DESK OF... Rodney

Now J.D. was crazy he was in bred
+ he drank whiskey like it was going out
you know I should of seen it coming
the writing was on the wall
he was getting just a little too loose
he made his mistake out on Airline
you know these North Houston cops are
they put a hole in J.D. the size of
+ took off my head with the
night stick

you know 5 to 10 in Huntsville
good time brothers but I walked
you know I mean
snug on that
Highway 17

FROM THE DESK OF... Rodney

I did my time the only way I knew
how thinking big + making plans
all about the ways I was gonna change my
world with my hands on that 15 grand

you know E.W. + Herschel my two oldest boys
took care of they mama + little sisters the
best way they could
dealing drugs + stealing hubcaps
they was doing good

I walked out that gate a free man
on November 22 1963
I kissed my wife + hugged the babies
but they didn't seem the same to me
you know they moved in cross the street
from the Chicken Police down at Lake City Square
they never bat an eye when they seen
you know they didn't even care
D H Bat

Highway 17 Revisited

I put away fifteen-grand doing one-night stands, mostly liquor stores and filling stations. Me and this peeping tom by the name of JD Swann and any number of his odd blood relations. This was armed robbery, nineteen-fifty-seven, and mostly our getaways were clean. I'd pay off the boys and bury my bread out on Highway 17.

I had five kids and a wife with one dress and a yard full of cars that would not run. My two oldest boys were on to my noise, they despised what their daddy'd done. But I did my thing the best I could making plans by the light of day. And then night would fall, it was time to call, and I was always on my way.

Now JD, he was crazy and he was inbred and he drank whiskey like it was going out of style. I should have seen it coming, the writing was on the wall, he was getting just a little too loose and wild. He made his mistake out on Airline Drive, you know those North Houston cops are quick. They blew a hole in JD the size of Dallas, and put a lump on my head with the brunt of a nightstick. You know that five-to-ten in Huntsville ain't no good time, boys, but I walked that line till . . . you know what I mean? My mind was snug on that hole I dug out on Highway 17. I said, my mind was snug on that hole I dug out on Highway 17.

So, I served my time the only way I knew how, thinking big and making plans. All about the way I was gonna change the world when I get my hands on that fifteen-grand. You know EW and Herschel, my two oldest boys, they took care of their mama and their little sisters the best way that they could—dealing dimes and stealing hubcaps, pretty soon they were doing good. I walked out those prison gates a free man on the first day of November, nineteen-and-sixty-three. I kissed my wife and I hugged my babies but they didn't seem the same to me. The boys looked on, they were already grown, it was written across their eyes and faces, I'm a perfect sample of a bad example, gone forever from their graces. But, baby, six long years and a lot can change many miles beyond your wildest dreams. But a six-lane-wide modern interstate ride out on Highway 17. Man, they sunk my ship beneath a concrete strip out on highway 17. They broke my back, they built a concrete track out on Highway 17. Lord, you know it ain't funny, they buried my money out on Highway 17.

Come On Funny Feeling

I don't want to wind up bitter, lost inside a silent rage
Or become like Rilke's panther out here locked up in a cage
The old man I've been talking to has cotton in his ears
But then who am I to blame him, I've had mine stopped up for years
Singing, come on funny feeling

LA out my windshield, one big Armageddon sprawl
Planting palm trees in the desert makes no sense to me at all
In a science fiction world where walkin' wounded leave their mark
I just took my place among them trying to find a place to park
Singing, come on funny feeling

The funny feeling comes when you're in love with everyone
And all your races have been run or laid to rest
So get this frickin' anvil off my chest . . . come on funny feeling

The funny feeling knows the way the whole thing comes and goes
Makes you stop and smell the roses if you're smart
So get this freakin' anvil off my heart . . . come on funny feeling

It's not like I'm not blessed with something special in this world
Just around the next dark corner there's a blue-eyed dancing girl
Who loves me like tomorrow comes with everything I need
I just have to pay attention where this road I'm on might lead
I'm thinkin' come on funny feeling

The funny feeling knows the truth, the eye for eye and tooth for tooth
It's something way back in your youth you should not second guess
The funny feeling never lies, it's there to open up your eyes
And make you stop and realize you're blessed
So get this frickin' anvil off my chest . . . come on funny feeling

(inspired by Steuart Smith)

I Don’t Care Anymore

I used to pull my britches on with just one thing in mind
Make the girls believe that I’m the last one of my kind
Silver toe tips on my boots and a mullet head of hair
Designed to walk into the room and make somebody stare
I don’t care anymore if I don’t stand out in a crowd
I was better off before I tried to make my mother proud

I came to town dreaming I could make my mark in spades
Forty-odd years later all my best cards have been played
It’s a hard-knock situation when the accolades bestowed
On your every last creation cries out “middle of the road”
I don’t care anymore about the fortune nor the fame
I was better off before I tried to make myself a name

All that money that I blew through like some boot-black off the farm
Could not have vanished quicker if I’d have shot it in my arm
Some so-and-so says, “Don’t you know the limit is the sky?”
The next thing I remember I’m unlearning how to fly
I don’t care anymore

All those party dolls and favors that I savored from day one
Add up to next to nothing after all is said and done
A real friend tried to tell me, man, with all respect it’s true
The time to put away these things is long since overdue

If indeed I do get lonesome in my mansion on the hill
There’s this neighbor’s wife I covet for her beauty and her skill
The way she puts herself together, sleek in vagabond couture
Makes each mailbox conversation one more heartache to endure
I don’t care anymore who does what and why
I was better off before when I was just another guy

I’ve been lied on, spied on, cried on, tried on, taken for a ride you bet
Fracked, cracked, smacked, Jack, what you see is what you get
I’ve been spit at, hit at, quit at, shit at, shouldn’t hurt a bit at, what I’m trying to get at
Fool me once, shame on me, fool me twice and put the blame on
I don’t care anymore
No, I don’t care anymore

Bradley Hartman, 1972

MORE BACK STORY 1965-75

I left home at age fifteen to join a rock and roll band named The Arbitrators and five years later formed a folk duo called Rodney & Donivan with my college roommate. His older brother, Walter Martin Cowart, was a pot-smoking, Bob Dylan-quoting poet, songwriter, and long-haul trucker and an instant role-model. His tales of the open road made the prospect of a degree in cultural anthropology, with a minor in political science—the only answer I could think of when a pretty co-ed asked what I was majoring in—even less appealing than assembling chicken coops for the Bright Coop Company, which is one of the ways Donivan and I managed to pay for the right to flunk out of Stephen F. Austin University. The other was playing cover songs in a half-empty Holiday Inn lounge.

In the spring of 1972, Rodney & Donivan got discovered by an alcoholic record producer from Pasadena, Texas, one of the incorporated cities contributing to Houston's greater sprawl. Within days we scurried off to Crowley, Louisiana, where he'd made arrangements to record an album of our woefully mediocre songs. When the dust settled on those sessions, my partner and I hurried back to our four-sets-a-night gig in an upscale steak house on the west side of Houston. In early August, I received a collect call from the long-silent producer with orders to round up Donivan and head for Nashville where a ten-year recording contract with Columbia Records and the opening slot on a year-long Kenny Rogers and the First Edition concert tour awaited our arrival. Around 3:00 a.m. on the morning after my twenty-second birthday, we rolled into Music City USA. The next three weeks were spent knocking on, and being turned away from, practically every door on what is known locally as Music Row. Nobody had ever heard of Rodney & Donivan. Meanwhile, no less than twenty of our collect calls to Pasadena went unanswered. Eventually, a songwriting friend of the producer's decided to drive up from Houston and fill in the blanks on what had become of our skyrocketing recording career. In a meeting that lasted no more than fifteen minutes, the amphetamine-wired associate explained our ever-sozzled producer, for the price of a bus ticket home, had sold our eight-track, master tapes and song-publishing rights to a company called Sure-Fire Music. And then, without bothering to divulge how he knew the tapes and contracts were sitting on top of a filing cabinet over at Sure-Fire, the guy popped another pill and headed back to Texas. The next day, Donivan and I cased out the company's building, and the day after that, during lunchtime, while he distracted the lonesome receptionist with small talk, I slipped the tapes and papers under my jacket, then we strolled out the door. This stolen property's still in my possession.

After the heist, the duo broke up when Donivan and the young wife he'd left waiting (semi-patiently) back in Texas decided to give Arizona a try. I opted to stick it out in Nashville, which involved continuing to sleep in my car, or on top of picnic tables scattered through the city's many parks. Thankfully, as the weather began turning cold, I ran into a pair of self-styled reprobates in the back room of Bishop's Pub, the only venue in town where a street-level songwriter

could sign up to play a twenty-minute set, pass the hat for tips, and, depending on how much beer he drank, walk away with a few bucks in his pocket. Luckily, the club owner's girlfriend took an interest in my well-being, and every night I played, she'd spot me a hamburger and pitcher of beer. With that and the five dollars I usually found in my hat, I was getting by.

One evening I was looking for an empty booth where I could enjoy my free supper when I noticed a six-foot-seven, one-hundred-and-forty-pound humanoid leaning on a que next to the pool table. As I passed by, he hocked up a giant loogie and spat it into in my beer. "You won't be needing any of this now, will ya?" Sneering, he grabbed the pitcher out of my hand and started glugging. I was surprised to hear myself say "I guess this means we're gonna be friends," and even more so when "Give me half of that hamburger and we'll see," was his response.

This, to my good fortune turned out to be Dennis Sanchez, an out-of-work upright bass player from Long Beach, California, who Guy Clark had already immortalized as Skinny Dennis in the song "L.A. Freeway."

Over the burger, he introduced me to his sidekick, Richard Dobson, who was a part-time bartender at the pub who wrote deceptively beautiful songs. Generally slow-moving, he was a Hemmingway disciple—complete with elbow patches on his tweed jacket. It turned out that he and Skinny Dennis needed some help with the rent on a two-bedroom house that happened to be within walking distance of the pub and, as luck would have it, the restaurant where I'd just stumbled onto a job as a dishwasher.

Overnight, that house on Acklen Avenue became a magnet for all the alternative-country, Texas blues, folk-rock and mainstream country singer/songwriters who, thanks to Kris Kristofferson's mega-success, were pouring into Nashville in the early seventies. That's where I met Guy and Susanna Clark, Townes Van Zandt, Mickey Newbury, Rocky Hill, Jim Maguire, David Allan Coe, Rex Bell, Harlan White, John Lomax III, David Olney, Mickey White, Steve Young, Johnny Rodriguez, Dave Loggins, Robin and Linda Williams, and Mayo

Thompson. More often than not, after getting off work around two in the morning, I'd walk home and find the house full of stoned songwriters hell-bent on one-upping one another with whichever song they'd just written and could barely remember the words to. A rare perk of late-shift dishwashing was the opportunity to finish off all the leftover half-empty cocktails, so most nights I stumbled home in the same shape as our drunken houseguests.

Bradley Harman

My first contribution to these get-togethers was a song my father taught me, "You Gotta Have a License." From then on, I was known as the guy who knew the words to more old songs than anybody else. Which might be why Guy Clark and I became fast friends.

Guy was the curator of this Acklen Avenue song-swapping salon, and I played a key role in his stewardship. When too many brand-new clunkers started grinding the party to a halt, Guy would call on me to play Chuck Berry's "Nadine," or an up-tempo sing-along like "My Home's Across the Blue Ridge Mountains" to get things moving again. As daybreak approached, it might be an Appalachian dead-baby song I'd learned from my dad or, even better, the not-so-subtle "Show Me the Way to Go Home." This knack allowed me to contribute without exposing how vapid my own compositions were at that time. Even more important was the chance to witness great songwriting up close. I was sitting two feet from Townes Van Zandt the first time I ever heard "Poncho and Lefty." Same goes for Dave Loggins's "Please Come To Boston."

Eventually, I moved on from Acklen Avenue. Around the same time, Guy and Susanna rented a cabin on Old Hickory Lake, and our growing friendship began having a lasting effect on my abilities as a songwriter. Guy was fond of making the point that for any dedicated writer—poet, novelist, songwriter, or journalist—getting better at what they do is the only measure of success. He put it to me like this: "Look, you can be a star, or you can be an artist. If rich and famous is what you're looking for, go on and knock yourself out. Just know that staying rich and famous will eventually involve putting your personality ahead of your art. If you pay attention only to the quality and integrity of the work, the money will eventually come. Probably just not as much as if you were a star."

Now and then, he'd play his prized recordings of Dylan Thomas reading *A Child's*

Christmas in Wales and *Under Milk Wood* and reiterate his belief that the words to a well-written song should sound as good read aloud as they do when sung. As time went on, and I started writing slightly better songs, if I thought I'd written something worthwhile, I would head over to Guy's house and---looking him square in the eye---recite the lyrics. Any impulse to turn away from his all-knowing gaze was the tell-tale sign that a line or couplet didn't make the cut. Occasionally, he'd drop by my place and do the same. This went on until the last few months of his life.

Susanna's influence was more intuitive. She became my muse. She'd already served as one, or would eventually, for many impressive songwriters, including Guy, Townes, Steve Earle, Lyle Lovett, Richard Leigh, and even, to some degree, Willie Nelson. While Guy and I often tried to bring the practicalities of songwriting—self-editing, narrative structure, and integrity—into focus, with Susanna it was all about the emotional experience. She was interested only in how a song made her feel. More or less by osmosis, I adopted her credo that a song should never draw attention to the mechanics involved in its creation. "I don't care how it's done, I only care what it does," is how she put it. As eager as I was to read new lyrics to Guy, I was even more keen to sing them to Susanna. Without her approval, a song simply wasn't a song.

By the winter of '73, I was holed up in a Hillsboro Village duplex with a new girlfriend—nicknamed, quite fittingly, Muffin—and my beloved dog, Banjo. A rumor going around town had Richard, my old housemate, living in the south of France, but in fact he was happily laying low in Lebanon, a small town east of Nashville, also with a new girlfriend, and working away on the next great American novel. Meanwhile, Skinny Dennis had hot-wired the one-room efficiency behind our apartment and was squatting there, Ratso Rizzo style, with his bass, a hot plate, and one change of clothes. The four of us (Banjo included) passed many bitter-cold evenings huddled around a pathetic little heater, eating brown rice and beans, and watching crappy black-and-white TV when we weren't listening to records. In those short gray days, I wrote "Bluebird Wine," "Song For The Life," and "An American Dream."

In early spring, a Nova Scotian bass player, Skip Beckwith, breezed into town hoping to convince a friend of mine to join him in Anne Murray's touring band. For reasons long since forgotten, their meeting took place in our apartment. After making a deal with his guitarist, the band leader then turned to me and asked if I had any new songs he could hear. Caught off- guard, I managed to play somewhat decent versions of the three I'd just written and, much to my surprise, he said he'd deliver a demo tape to his boss up in Toronto.

The songs never reached Anne Murray. Her producer, Brian Ahern, was also working on Emmylou Harris's debut album. As she later told me, they'd wasted several days playing demo tapes without hearing a single song she could imagine recording. As a last resort, Ahern pulled out a reel-to-reel demo a bass-playing friend had given him a couple of months before. The first song on this tape was "Bluebird Wine," which wound up being the opening track on Emmylou's *Pieces of the Sky*.

For much of the late summer and fall of '74, I was in Toronto. But just before Thanksgiving, believing central Texas was where I'd spend the rest of my life, I rented an apartment in Austin. Then, in January, Emmylou called to say she and the Angel Band would be playing at the Armadillo World Headquarters in a few days and that she was hoping I'd sing a couple of songs with her. After the show, she casually mentioned that she was flying out to Los Angeles the next morning and thought, since she just happened to have a spare ticket, it would be great if I wanted to come along. (Such were the days when an unknown songwriter could fly across the country on somebody else's ticket.) I eventually found out that her manager, Eddie Tickner, had convinced Warner Bros. Records to give their promising new artist enough money to pull together a high-powered touring outfit. As it happened, half of its members were on loan from Elvis Presley's famous TCB Band, but I'd been her first recruit.

Meanwhile, Skinny Dennis had returned to Southern California and was backing up a folksinger named John Penn. I'd been in LA only a month or two when I heard he'd collapsed onstage at a Long Beach folk club and was dead before he hit the floor. Would I mind being a pallbearer the caller asked.

At the funeral, I learned from a family member that the cause of my friend's physical abnormalities, and perhaps even his heart-attack, was a genetically-inherited disease known as the Marfan Syndrome, which affects the cardiovascular system and skeletal structure of its victims. I also learned that Dennis's family members were descendants of an Indian tribe in northern Mexico whose adult males averaged five-feet-four-inches in height. This explained why I was a full head taller than most people there, and also clarified something Dennis often said that I'd never fully understood: "I'm as long on lonesome and ugly as my people are short on tall."

After I said goodbye to my old bass playing friend, I hit the road as a member of Emmylou Harris's Hot Band.

Dan Reeder

he Schaefer
usic Festival
Central Park
TH

Gary P.Nunn

Dan Reeder

western union Mailgra

MS. HANNAH CROWELL
823 MONTERRY BLVD
HERMOSABEACH CA 90254

GREETINGS TAURUS
REMIND DAD T MAKE HIS FLIGHT ON THE 10TH LOVE AND LUCK
EMMY AND THE HOT BAND

13:04 EST

Dan Reeder

Willie

EMMYLOU HARRIS
&
THE HOT BAND
The
United Kingdom
Tour
February '76

THE WARNER BROS MUSIC SHOW
WB

Fucking
Brilliant
JOURNAL

SELECTED LYRICS
PART TWO

Nashville 1972

I had a dog named Banjo and a girl named Muffin
I just blew in from Texas, I didn't know nothin'
But I found my way around this town with a friend I made named Guy
Who loved Susanna, and so did I

Now there was this run-down shack on Acklen Avenue that I shared with Skinny Dennis
And a poet name of Richard Dobson who had a novel he'd never finish
That's when Johnny Rodriguez and David Olney and Steve Earle first came through
And every other guitar bum whose name I never knew

Old school Nashville, Harlan Howard, Bob McDill
Tom T. Hall, go drink your fill and blow us all away

There was this tight-rope-walker who called herself the queen of Poughkeepsie
Who ran away from the circus with some roustabout redneck gypsy
They were Townes Van Zandt fans and prone to combustion
They fought like dogs in Spanish and made love in Russian

I wish Newberry and Buck White would drop on by the house tonight
Things have changed 'round here, you bet, but it don't seem much better yet

I first met Willie Nelson with some friends at a party
I was twenty-two years old, and he must have been pushing forty
There was hippies and reefer and God knows what all, I was drinking pretty hard
I played him this shitty song I wrote, then puked out in the yard

Old school Nashville, Harlan Howard, Bob McDill
Tom T. Hall, go drink your fill and blow us all away
Tom T. Hall, go drink your fill and blow us all away

Life Without Susanna

Life without Susanna started when Townes Van Zandt died
From that day on she hid out undercover
Her Percocet and cigarette along for the ride

She made the bed inside her head a shelter
Each new day a sliver through the blind
I tried tough love, tenderness and anger
But nothing pierced the fortress inside her mind

The first time I saw her she threw me that smile
Pure angel of mercy, east Texas style
A poet in gingham, an assassin in jeans
The most near-perfect woman that I'd ever seen
She was hardly routine

Life without Susanna troubles me in ways hard to express
As she withdrew I grew distant and judgmental
A self-sure bastard and a stubborn bitch
Locked in a deadly game of chess
The upside of my status, a cut above the rest

The last time I saw her was close to the end
I cried like a baby for the shape she was in
No lipstick or powder could soften the tone
The most worthy opponent I've ever known
Was already gone

Life without Susanna is something that we all have to face
So, welcome to the world as we don't know it
Big blue knuckleball free-floating somewhere out in space
Where life without Susanna is no man's saving grace
This is life without Susanna and I can't find my place

Riding Out the Storm

The New York City winter comes in cold grey sheets of steel
The numbness in his hands and feet is all that he can feel
Alcohol and Sterno turns a doorway to a bed
And the ghost of who he might have been lives on inside his head

In a canyon made of brownstone on a sidewalk icy black
He wanders nearly barefoot with his righteousness intact
A man of many mansions in a cardboard box replete
Lies sleeping with an angel while his heart pretends to beat
The wind blows down on lonely street like an ice pick through the air
Amidst the Sunday Times and coffee grinds and winos in Times Square
Five flights up on easy street you know she's safe and warm
Way down low 'neath a foot of snow he's riding out the storm

I offered him my winter coat, politely he refused
Like an educated man he spoke with words I seldom use
He said, "I don't need pity, these choices are my own"
He bowed his head just slightly then quietly moved along
The wind blows down on lonely street like an ice pick through the air
Amidst the Sunday Times and coffee grinds and winos in Times Square
Five flights up on easy street you know she's safe and warm
Way down low 'neath a foot of snow he's riding out the storm

It's not like he's a victim of this homeless life he stalks
Nor helpless to get back across the fine line that he walks
Riding out the storm means yesterday's already spent
Tomorrow don't mean nothing, it won't even make a dent
The wind blows down on lonely street like an ice pick through the air
Amidst the Sunday Times and coffee grinds and winos in Times Square
Five flights up on easy street you know she's safe and warm
Way down low 'neath a foot of snow he's riding out the storm

The Girl on the Street

She spied me through the traffic and was on me in a flash
Some soft soak out-of-towner and an easy mark for cash
In contrast to her ragged cloak of filth and disrepair
Was a dark-eyed mystic beauty and a raven shock of hair
With what was feral frantic motion, her every move was laced
With the kind of desperation born of demons not yet faced
Quite clearly, she was hounded by some not-too-distant past
That was feasting on each moment like it just might be her last
    The girl on the street was once somebody's daughter
    Yeah, the girl on the street was once somebody's friend
    The girl on the street, one more lamb led to the slaughter
    Where for three dimes and a quarter she gets nothing in the end

She hit me up with hunger, first things first, you know
But a little too coquettish for my sympathy to show
She offered up her favors with a nod below the belt
And a parting shot at pity for the cards that she'd been dealt
"It's dope," said I, "be truthful, it's right there in your eyes
You know that stuff will kill you, it's a loaded pack of lies"
She rolled her sleeve, slapped her vein and spat out, "Three months clean
Hey, don't pretend you know me, man, just cough up something green"
    The girl on the street was once somebody's daughter
    Yeah, the girl on the street was once somebody's friend
    The girl on the street finds you tailor-made to order
    And for three dimes and a quarter you get nothing in the end

So, with the loose change in my pocket, I let myself off light
When I could have helped her find some food and shelter for the night
Compassion for the dope-sick twenty-something whore
Hit way too close to home for me to open up that door
So please don't say, "Go easy, man, so what if you came up short?"
I might have made a difference if I'd only had the heart
    The girl on the street was once somebody's daughter
    Yeah, the girl on the street was once somebody's friend
    The girl on the street, in spite of everything you taught her,
    Gone for three dimes and a quarter and you still lose her in the end

I saw her first & judged her
Close to 30 not much more
Pretty way untreated
As much Schizophrenic dancer

Pretty Dopesick junkie whore

Her skin was p
Her clothes were caked with filth

Dopesick junkie off the block

Her clothes were homeless ragged
Her skin was caked with layered filth

But her skin was caked & filthy

On second glance I noticed
something

I saw her first and judged
her just some Dopesick
Junkie whore
But something said look
closer & you might see
something more

Her clothes were torn & ragged

On second glance I noticed
something such a lovely head of hair
In contrast to the ragged filth
The ~~homeless~~ & homeless wear
Her ragged cloak of filth &
stark despair

I stood there for a moment thinking
Next I caught her movements
like a dancer's lightly graced
& I wondered was she chasing or

was it she who's being chased

Clearly there were demons

Clearly there were demons
In a not-to-distant past
~~But something~~ feasting on tomorrow
like it just might be her
I stood there on the corner last
Leavenworth & Golden Gate
and marveled at this creature
In her agitated state

~~When~~
Suddenly she turned on me

and as if by psychic radar she

She was lost
Frantic movement
Frantic dancer

I saw her first & judged her
Close to 30 not much more
untreated schizophrenic
or Some Dopesick junkie whore
was
On second glance I noticed
was shreds of recent beauty
Such a lovely head of hair
on her face & in hair
In contrast to her ragged cloak

of filth and stark despair
were the remnants of a beauty
Next I caught her movements
like a dancer's lightly graced
was there something she was chasing
or was it she who's being chased
Clearly there were demons
from some not-to-distant past
Feasting on tomorrow like it just
might be her last
motion
She was lost in frantic movement
But with natural dancers grace

FERAL

and so I lingered on the corner
of Leavenworth & Golden Gate
The ~~[illegible]~~
& marveled at this creature
In her agitated state

She was lost in frantic motion
~~But with~~ every move was
yet her ~~movement~~ graced
movement laced
She might have been a dancer

But for the demons that she
faced

The ease of self expression
In spite of demons that she
faced
Her dancers grace her pretty face
& perfect head of hair

She was lost in frantic motion
yet her every move was laced
with ease of self expression
Despite demons that she faced

Clearly she was haunted by some
not-to-distant past
Feasting on tomorrow like it
just might be ~~her~~ last

The girl on the street
was once somebody's daughter
" " " "
was once somebody's friend

Secret desperation
like some demon that she faced

~~Some~~ As if by psychic radar
She must have known my
She sensed that I was there

She picked up on my drift
& threw her head up in the
air
feral
In all of San Francisco

Hit me up for money
She said she needed money

In contrast to her ragged cloak
of filth & stark despair
was her dancers grace, her pretty
face & perfect head of hair

As I lingered on the corner
of Post & Golden Gate
& marveled at this creature
In her agitated state

As if by psychic power or some
~~feral drift~~
Telepathic drift
She picked up on my wavelength
& I ~~[illegible]~~ watched her body shift
She threw her head up in the air
& craned her neck to hear

Just who this soft intruder
was who whispered in her ear

She spied me through the traffic
~~& Cross~~ & with that she
~~Crossed the line~~ stretched the
flow & was on me in a blink
& I   like a flash
Distant recognition in an easy
mark for cash

She hit me up ~~for money~~ with hunger
First things first   ~~I~~ no doubt you know
A little too coquettish for
~~my empathy to share~~
for the tenderness to share
She offered me her favors
with a nod below the belt

The boulevards of San Francisco
Leavenworth & Golden Gate
I marveled at this creature
in her agitated state
As if by psychic power or some hidden power
Telepathic drift
She picked up on my wavelength
& I felt her body shift

She threw her head up in the air
& craned her neck to hear see
~~the~~ just who this soft intruder
was that whispered in her ear
+ what his game might be
She spied me through the traffic (him)
& was on me in a flash
~~One more~~ Leavenworth out-of-towner
~~& an easy mark~~ for cash

One more redneck out of town
One more easy mark for cash

She hit me up with hunger
First things first you know
But a little too coquettish
for the tenderness to place
So she offered me her favors
with a nod (below) below the belt
& bid me show some pity
For the cards that she'd been
dealt

I said why not be truthful
It's crack you want to buy
It's another fix you crave
The very thing that'll lead you to
an early unmarked grave
With that you'd think I'd
~~hit~~ smacked her with a brick
between the eyes
She did her best to compose up

Some long forgotten tears

She rolled her sleeve
slapped her vein & cried
I'm ~~been~~ clean for days

It's drugs I said be truthful
Why can't you just be truthful
I said   I see it in your eyes

You know that stuff will kill you

It's drugs I said be truthful
It's written on your face
You know that stuff will kill you
It's an empty hole you chase

She rolled her sleeve & slapped her vein
And spat out ~~clean for weeks~~
Look who's clean

~~You don't even fuckin know me~~
I'm 7 years now clean
Hey don't pretend you know
me ~~you~~ just cough up
something green

Clean for 7 years

Three quarters and a dime
Is all I came up with that
day
& I have to say I'm sorry
That it al

Helped her find someplace to stay
It's not like I believe
~~It~~ could have made a difference
But I just can't shake the feeling
That I let her get away
I guess
Tenderness
That I threw away

Could have been my daughter
~~or~~ somebody's friend

I wish I'd bought her dinner
or offered her
Given her a bath
or seen she had a bath

Was once somebody's lover
Was once somebody's friend
Small change in my pocket
Three quarters & a dime
Is all I chose to give her
When I could have bought
her dinner & helped offered her
Find a bath   Helped find a room somewhere
~~Although~~ It's not like I believe
That it would have made a
difference
But just can't shake the feeling

Could have been my daughter
Perhaps my daughter's friend

She came into my life
like a blessing made to order

& for three dimes & a quarter
I lost her to the [illegible]
I cast her to the wind
I can't go back again
Could have been
Somebody's sister
Or somebody's sister's
friend

Seems I failed her on the [illegible]

The blessings in my life
tailor made to order

Down on Leavenworth & Golden Gate

Just wanted to see you
Day [illegible]
[illegible]
When the war is over
The girl on the street
You got lucky
Call me up
Walk across town
She ain't gonna [illegible]
7 shades of blue

One Little Bird

When I was a child an inch was a mile, each passing day felt like a year
And now I'm here where time is fleet, it's short but sweet and that seems fair
Along the way, I have to say, I caused some hurt that I can't mend
And to that end I came up short, if I were smart I'd have left it right there

There's this one little bird in the tree outside my door
And she's singing a song that goes right to the core
She says, "Where will you go, where will you be?
Why don't you know, why can't you see it's almost over?"

I've seen the end of a rainbow through a Greyhound window
Blue northern lights 'cross a prairie sky
When a drink of cool water from a dried-up mountain spring
Says as much about anything as the fifth of July
You need to ask yourself why

The name is Crowell, no harm no foul, unless of course I've been unkind
With that in mind I rest my case, your axe to grind is my saving grace
And I've been put in my place

By this one little bird in all the trees outside my door
And she's singing a song that cuts right to the core
She says, "Where will you go, where will you be?
Why don't you know, why can't you see it's almost over?"

RODNEY CROWELL

PONTE VEDRA CONCERT HALL
SUN. MARCH 6, 2022 · 8:00 PM

Transient Global Amnesia Blues

A sunflower growing on a narrow raft in a fog bank on the Thames
Adrift above the tide-slime where nothing holy swims
Wherever did it come from, likely bird shit someone said
Just a random freak of nature that refuses to play dead
Oh, to be that stand up straight, past seven feet or more
She ain't no faux silk pansy, boys, what washed up on the shore
So, let us stop and marvel for as long as we can spare
Seems you have no need for heaven when your heart's already there
        Would that I should be so bold, greatest story never told
        Worth the wait in solid gold, would that I should be so bold

I dreamed on Sunshine Skyway Bridge 'tween Tampa and St. Pete
Titanic and the iceberg, and the twain still yet to meet
I was running long-side Jesus Christ, plumed helmet and red cape
When I vowed unto the Prince of Peace to aid in his escape
When I felt the spear go in me from the right side to the left
I was streaming "Mississippi" (see Bob Dylan, *Love and Theft*)
When Jesus turned to thank me for the gift of second sight
I waved him off, "No worries, man, I think I'll be alright."
        Would that I were born again, makes no difference where or when
        Knowing now what I knew then, would that I were born again

From where the rainbow eucalyptus stand beyond the river Styx
To the Blood Falls in the Arctic, it's at least eight thousand clicks
You can get there as the crow flies headed north from Singapore
But you better get a move on 'fore she melts down to the core
Though a red dawn in an angry sky portends blue rue and ruin
It's that want-to-be-a-rich-guy who pretends there's nothing doing
But if that ticking time bomb beneath the Yellowstone should blow
It's adios, amigo, see you somewhere down below
        Would that we should e'er forget things that haven't happened yet
        That someday we might regret, would that we should e'er forget

RC 10-9-20

If it serves some greater purpose

To serve your greater purp
In the form of mystic deed
My will be done in your name lo

Here goes nothing unlike every time
This time it could be different this time there
This time the stars could fall in line for rea
A gift of one more second chance to make
Where the righteous claim their dignity
I hope someday to be there live among you

Here goes nothing tired of nothing le
On a road in search of meaning use
If it serves some truth can allay I'll and
I'm ready for to go there I'll do anything
To serve some greater purpose to hea

In ~~Youth~~ ~~Song~~

...e

Perform your mystic deed

No matter what that comes

Before

Could be more

...s of their own

...y Purpose Know

...e meek are truly blessed

Heaven's Guests

... to Go

...e any way you choose

...n Forgotten Land

... call

...one higher call

To serve some
greater purpose
Perform one
single deed
Thy will be done
In your name
Lord

By fate of mystic
deed

Here Goes Nothing

If only I could see myself through your eyes for a day
I wonder just how I might fare when love comes into play
I know that I don't give as much as I so often take
I guess it's just old habit keeps me putting on the brake

If only I could see it all less darkly through the glass
A world yet unimagined soon must surely come to pass
And when instead of shadows, light comes shining through
Perhaps I'll find forgiveness for the things I can't undo

Here goes nothing, I've got nothing left to lose
I'm a man in search of meaning, use me any way you choose
If it serves some greater purpose by fate or simple deed
Thy will be done in your name, I'll go anywhere you lead
Here goes nothing, I've got nothing left to lose
Ooh ya ya oh ooh ya yay a ya yay Ooh ya ya oh my Lord ooh ya ya ya ya yay

If only I could take it in from somewhere out in space
Some otherworldly port of call, some future time and place
Where the things that really matter have no tether to the past
And in each and every moment I'm a free man born at last

Here goes nothing, unlike every time before
This time it could be different, this time there could be more
This time the stars could fall in line for reasons yet untold
A gift of one more second chance to come in from the cold
Whereby providence and mercy lost and ragged souls are blessed
I hope someday to be there, Lord, among your honored guests
Here goes nothing, I've got nothing left to lose
Ooh yay ya oh ooh ya ya ya ya yay ooh ya ya oh my Lord ooh ya ya ya ya yay

Triage

I think I know what love is, forgiveness for a start
Room for those you love to hate somewhere inside your heart
There are those who say that love is naught but gossip column news
Or old roller skates that fasten to the bottom of your shoes
Love

Some say love's a meditation on everything we are
Good, bad, and indifferent, self-righteous and bizarre
It's right there in the crosshairs, our every last mistake
The sinners we've made holy, the saints we've burned at stake

If love is revelation and love we thus receive
It all comes down to knowing less than most of us alone believe

If you're asking me what love is, here's what I might say
You can find it out there anywhere on any given day
It's an endless stream of consciousness obtained in drips and drabs
And a chance to do the right thing when there's no one keeping tabs

If love is what we make it, as you reap so you sow
The yang and yen, the where and when, the first and last to come and go
If love is all creation, love is manifest
It's love when we're all given life, and love when we're all laid to rest

(for Joe Henry)

Claudia Church

Reckless

Last night I lay dreaming I was drinking in a hotel bar
Two women came up and kissed me, and you were watching from a distant star
I know it doesn't make much sense but what can I tell you?
Judging by the evidence, I'm feeling reckless

I don't know why I would go there all to make a fuss, over what?
I've got a woman like you and what do I do, pretend I might be something I'm not
I know you know it's not your fault, it's just something inside me
Would that I were worth my salt, but I'm feeling reckless

You give me more than I deserve, you could say I've got some nerve

So, slay me with your tender mercy, comfort me with words of steel
You can catch me in a lie when I cast a roving eye but you'll never know the way I feel
I know you know you're smarter than me, tell me something I don't know
There's so much more that I could be but I'm feeling reckless

I Wouldn't Be Me Without You

Sometimes I think about leaving, and If I had some place to go
I might even crank up the engine and roll down the street just for show
Nobody said it was easy but that doesn't mean it ain't right
I don't want nobody else with me when it comes time to call it a night

So far I've kept every promise, and this I'll continue to do
I'll love you like nobody's business, I wouldn't be me without you

I don't need the rain to remind me how good it feels to come clean
The worst of the past put behind me are spoken words I didn't mean
If I have to tell you I'm sorry for something I shouldn't have done
It won't be for some other woman who smiles like she thinks I'm someone

So far I've kept every promise and this I'll continue to do
I'll love you, come hell or high water, I wouldn't be me without you
No, I wouldn't be me without you

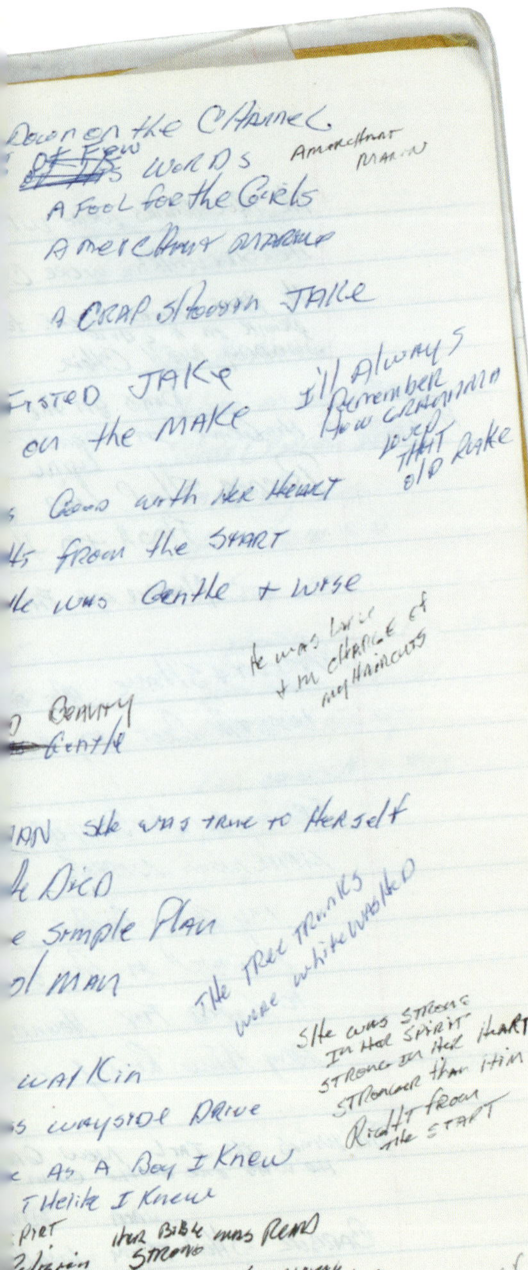

Grandma Loved That Old Man

My grandfather wore big suspenders
A grey fedora hat, shine on his shoes
Tobacco stains on his chin
Gin on his breath, and starch in his shirts

He always had change in his pockets
A watch in his vest, a tie tacked to his chest
He was crap-shooting crazy, a hungover lazy wrestling match fan
I'll never forget how my grandma loved that old man

He was a night watchman down on Canal Street
A salty old bird, a man of few words
He was Friday night vain, he walked with a cane
Smoked Prince Albert in a can
I'll never forget how my grandma loved that old man

She was strong in her spirit, strong in her heart
Loved that old man right from the start
Sometimes I did wonder how much she could take
She was pushed to the limit but she never did break
Her life followed one simple plan, Grandma loved that old man

His tree trunks were white washed, sidewalks were clean
Beer joints were crawling with merchant marines
He went to his grave with a barbershop shave and his dice in his hand
I'll never forget how my grandma loved that old man
I'll never forget how much Grandma loved that old man

Whitewash is Gone from the tree trunks
Sidewalks are Busted & the street signs are Rusted

Rounder

Grandpa was a ~~Nigh~~ Rounder

~~A~~ A Night watchman on the Ship Chanel

Merchant Marines where part of the scene

Houston was hard in the ~~80's~~ Good ~~ay~~ Lord

Merchant Marines Drank to extreemes

~~Grandpa the~~ Dice the dice Games were

salty ol Birds
Merchant Marines
Dice shootin Fools
New Animal name

Grandpa wore ~~th~~ suspenders

Fedora Hat shine on his shoes

Tobacco juice on his chin Gin on his Breath

Starch ~~on~~ in his shirt

He was a Rounder

A Night watchman + a Merchant Marine

Houston was hard Rollin back then

+ He was a Rambler

Grandma was Good with her Hands

she could sew she could cook Could Read me a Book

she could teach me to pray she could make

He Always had change in his pocket

A watch ~~in~~ in his vest Grease in his hair a tooth in his eye teeth in a glass Fox Hounds to Run

A pint on his hip and the wrestlin matches

I'll never forget just how much

I Loved that old man

He was a Night watchman Down on the Channel

Houston was hard in the 40's Good Lord

Them ol merchant marines Dice shootin Fakes

salty ol Birds

Stars on the Water

Down in Louisiana, bayou's by and by
A peirrot pole and your natural soul keep you tied to a tree-high tide
Beer joint lights come on and then the crowd starts rolling in
Pretty soon you've got stars on the water, stars on the water, stars on the water
Let it rain

Beaumont to Biloxi, sea breeze at your door
Gypsy rain, hurricane, white silver sandy shore
Blue light lounge shining way out on the pier
It looks just like stars on the water, stars on the water, stars on the water
Let it rain

When it's midnight down in Mobile, shining moonbeams on the bay
They come from miles around to dance a jukebox down
To hear the good time sounds they all play
All across the harbor, nightlife shining on
Like stars on the water, stars on the water, stars on the water
Let it rain

STARS ON THE WATER R. Crowell

Down in Louisiana Bayou's By & By
A Pirot Pole or your natural soul
Keeps you tied to a tree high tide
Beer Joint Lights come on & then the crowd starts rollin in
Pretty soon you got Stars on the Water
Stars on the Water
Stars on the Water Let it Rain

Beaumont to Biloxi Seabreeze at your door
Gypsy Rains Dang Hurricanes White Silver Sandy Shores
Blue Light Lounge is Shinin Way out on the Pier
Makes it Look just Like Stars on the Water
Stars on the Water
Stars on the Water If it Rains

When its Midnight Down in Mobile
Shinin Moon beams on the Bay
They come from miles around to dance the Juke Box down
& Dig the Good Time sounds they all play
All across the Harbor Nightlife Shinin On
Looks just Like Stars on the Water
Stars on the Water
Stars on the Water
Make it Rain

—0— 79-81

Tennessee Wedding

Let's mock despair with food and wine, tango like we're Argentine
While in our wake rose petals rise and fall
With expectation in full bloom we'll cast ourselves as bride and groom
What love has joined together says it all
Life's beauty pageant queen of hearts blows kisses from her horse-drawn cart
With scented breath and gloved white hand, your every wish her soft command

When we arrive as honored guests where John and June were laid to rest
In Tennessee, the land that gave you life
We'll stand before those near-and-dear, and speak these words for all to hear
From now until forever be my wife
Your father's arm, a hallowed "yes," to wear your mother's wedding dress
With a parasol and walking cane, we'll set our course down lover's lane

Marry me, my dark eyed pearl, my raven-haired country girl
Marry me, and we'll sail away home

When another round of day and night blinks off and on like Christmas lights
Each parting shot fired low across the bow
With each new breath, a ray of hope we'll grieve our losses fully yoked
To life's eternal passing into now
For generations long since gone and those yet born, we'll soldier on
Till kingdom come and then some, I promise to be true to you
Marry me, my dark-eyed swan, my morning star, my evening sun
Marry me, and we'll sail away home

(for Carrie and Daniel)

Sex and Gasoline

So much beauty, abs and tush swoop down on you like a burning bush
Pop religion, bullwhip thin, says you ain't nothing but the shape you're in
Come on, little girl, genuflect nude magazine, this mean old world runs on
Sex and gasoline

Nineteen candles adorn your cake, life's simple pleasures is the chance you take
Here's the skinny, indulge the urge, then sometime later you can binge and purge
Come on, little girl, we both know what I mean, this mean old world runs on
Sex and gasoline

You're pushing thirty, why you old hag, here's something dirty for your shopping bag
You spend the money, here's the deal, we'll do our best to mend your sex appeal
Come on, dear girl, the process is routine, this mean old world runs on
Sex and gasoline

You're over forty, that's it for you, I'm pretty sure there's nothing left that we can do
Perhaps the convent, perhaps the knife, you could-a should-a been a rich man's wife
Come on, old girl, Lolita in her prime was yet thirteen, this mean old world runs on
Sex and gasoline

Tired old story, sad but true, we mama's boys have got it in for you
Our faults are many, virtue's nil, we never loved you and we never will
Ah, come on now, girl, it's time we both come clean, this mean old world runs on
Sex and gasoline
From the first-grade princess to the last homecoming queen this mean old world runs on
Sex and gasoline
Oh yes and your mother's world ran on
Sex and gasoline

I've Done Everything I Can, There's Nothing I Can Do

I'd love to hear you laughing, love to see you smile
Dance that little dance you danced when you were just a child
The way the world came at you left you bitter and confused
The more I tried to guide your path, the more you just felt used
The sun comes up tomorrow but there are no guarantees
It can rock you like a baby, it can knock you to your knees
The path that lies between us is a star-crossed avenue
I've done everything I can, there's nothing I can do

> So, you love that girl to death, and you're scared to take a breath
> It's like everything you dread swings a hammer in your head
> So, her heart's locked in a vault, and you think it's all your fault
> It's a dream as old as dirt, you can't stand to see her hurt

May the little voice that guides you bring a message through from me
Reminding you you're beautiful, and will forever be
I wish that I could be there now to tell you it's alright
It's a dark and daunting razor's edge you're walking on tonight
The sun comes up tomorrow but there are no guarantees
It can rock you like a baby, it can knock you to your knees
The path that lies between us is a rough and rocky rue
I've done everything I can there's nothing I can do

> So, you're learning to let go, and the process is so slow
> While your baby plumbs the depths, you keep climbing up the steps
> She was daddy's little girl, you were ruler of the world
> Now she's out there in the fray, ah but she'll be back some day

You've heard me say a million times, my work is never done
For those who keep the wolves at bay there is no setting sun
To see you standing here today, pray child you've come so far
Which proves that you can find your way no matter where you are

The sun comes up tomorrow but there are no guarantees
It can rock you like a baby, it can knock you to your knees
The path that lies between us is the long way home, it's true
I've done everything I can, and there's nothing I can do
I've done everything I can, now it's up to you

I Know Love is All I Need

So, I'm an orphan now out here on my own, and it's hard to know where I belong
It comes as no surprise, it happens to us all, just like the sun will rise, night will fall

I know love is all I need, I know love is all I need
I know love is all I need, that's all I know

An image I recall, a picture on my wall of my mother on her wedding day
Young and naïve, nothing up her sleeve but the things that just got lost along the way

I know love is all I need, I know love is all I need
I know love is all I need, that's all I know

There's a voice I hear, it comes in loud and clear, it's my father's voice teaching me
He says to be a man you've got to be true to your word, and when you make a stand
You'll be heard

I know love is all I need, I know love is all I need
I know love is all I need, that's all I know

I can see it in my children, I can feel it with my wife
And I know it with these friends I have who are so important to my life

I had a dream last night, I saw my ma and dad
they were happy now and I was glad
They had this brand-new house that they'd just moved in
and when I awoke they were gone again

But I know love is all I need
I know love is all I need
I know love is all I need
That's all I know

Closer to Heaven

I don't like Hummers, I hate long lines
Nosey neighbors and Venetian blinds
Chirpy news anchors alter my mood
I'm offended by buzzwords like awesome and dude
I look like a train wreck, I feel like a blob
Till you get to know me you may think I'm a snob
But I'm closer to heaven than I've ever been

I don't eat sushi, I don't smoke grass
I don't wear pajamas, I don't drive fast
I hate idle gossip and tasseled shoes
Slick politicians give me the blues
I don't ride in limos, I can't play golf
I don't own a rifle that will blow your head off
But I'm closer to heaven than I've ever been

I'm riding that wave from cradle to grave
I'm learning to feel my hands on the wheel

I love my friends, I love my wife
Four little babies are the light of my life
I love Sissy Spacek, I love Guy Clark
All the biscuits and gravy I can eat with a fork
I don't want to be famous, who gives a damn?
I just want to be happy whoever I am
And I'm closer to heaven than I've ever been

I'm learning to feel my hands on the wheel

Dirty Dishes

I don't want to die til I learn how to fly

I don't like limo's

I'm riding the wave from cradle to grave
At long last I feel my hands on the wheel
The closer I get the less I regret

I don't like hummus I hate long lines
Despise nosy neighbors & Venetian blinds
I hate leaky faucets I don't like cats
& I feel like a cheese ball in a house full of rats
Reality T.V. gives me the creeps
I'm offended by buzz words like chop chop & peeps
I look like a train wreck I feel like a blob
Til you get to know me you'd think I'm a snob

I don't eat sushi I don't smoke grass
I don't wear pajamas I don't drive fast
Slick politicians get on my nerves
I don't love/lend money I don't play golf
I don't own a rifle that'll blow your head off
I hate ~~gossip columns~~ potty gossip & fast track news
[illegible] & [illegible] just gimme the blues

I pay my taxes I drink red wine
If I mind my own business it all will be fine

A gift from the sea
High school football H.B.O
Kind hearted people and dogs running free

I don't need to be happy I don't want to be cool
I don't have to be ready

I don't like the color red

I love my friends I love my cat I love my [illegible] I love my wife
I don't like neckties
I like good hummus - I hate long lines nosy neighbors
& Venetian blinds

I hate dripping faucets I don't like cats
Sometimes I'm a cheese ball in a world full of rats
& love good hummus I crave facial hair
I have been known to hug a tree I've been known to stare
I don't like whisky I don't smoke grass
The drug of my choice is a good piece of ass
I love Fort Worth I hate
I don't eat sushi I don't play golf
I don't wear pajamas
I have boundary problems I don't play golf
I don't have issues and agenda per se

I love Sissy Spacek I love Guy Clark
I love all the catfish I can eat with a fork
I have never lied to when I'm hammered And I hate when I lie
I hate when I'm cruel
when I try to be cool
I look like a & I feel like a [illegible]

The closer I get the sweeter the song
It's not over yet but it won't be that long

Something Has to Change

Two kids at a stoplight wiping windshields in the snow
Sticking close together now, trying to make a go
In a nickel and dime world it's catch as catch can
If you've never been there you won't understand

It's greed, it's not money, through which evil works
The haves and the have nots are just one of the perks
Where life has a purpose, faith has a voice
We can't live in fear like this and in trembling rejoice

Someday, someway, something has to change

Am I ready for times such as these? Emphatically no
Though I did see it coming a long time ago
Way out in the cosmos, past its never-ending swirl
There's a power much greater than those that would
darken the world

Someday, somehow, something has to change

painting by Ray Martin

You Cant Keep me Here IN TENNESSEE Rodney Crowell 23.

By the time we left Kentucky All that was on my mind
was the way I spend my trouble like A Dime
When we Got Back to Nashville things were still the Same
+ All my thoughts Ran Back To Texas, IN Hopes to Ease the Pain
Cause you fall like A TREE when your Cut Down
youve Been to Long Hacking Away At me
Its A Long old Road Im taking back to Texas
Cause you can't Keep me Here IN TENNESSEE
IN All my Looking At you, its funny all the things Ive Never seen
Cause the sun Dont shine beside you Leastwise It Aint Never
shone on me (shone on me)
Cause you fall like A tree when your Cut down
And youve been too long Hacking Away at me
Its A long old Road Im taking Back to Texas
Cause you cant Keep me Here IN Tennessee
my minds been IN A Dungeon, Prisoner IN your world of make believe
Im Begging for your Pardon Ive served my time so now Ill take my
Leave (Take my Leave)
Cause you fall like A tree when your Cut Down
youve been too Long Hacking Away At me
Its A Long old Road Im Taking Back to Texas
Cause You Cant Keep me Here IN Tennessee

FIRST TASTE OF SUCCESS

Maybe six months after I arrived in Nashville, I met a girl who offered to share her bed as occasional solace from the never-ending hubbub on Acklen Avenue. Around the same time, Harlan White asked if I'd help make the most of the studio time he'd somehow managed to book at Jack Clement's Studio B. I was, more or less, named his unofficial producer. Guy Clark, Susanna Clark, and Townes Van Zandt got wind of the session and sent word they'd probably be dropping by. I also invited my intermittent girlfriend to join the party. The more absorbed I became in getting Harlan's songs on tape, the less aware I was of the social maneuvers going on behind my back. Had I known the studio was equipped with a hidden, state of the art, black-light-and-hippie-poster lounge, chances are I'd have paid more attention to my date for the evening. But it wasn't until the next day, when Susanna broke the news to me that Townes had used the lounge to seduce my girlfriend, that the blinders came off. The speed with which I went from big-shot demo producer to turnip-truck bumpkin was breathtaking. I spent the rest of the day pouring my shame and anger into a song about getting the hell out of Dodge.

A week before the infamous session, I landed the happy hour gig at a bar and restaurant called the Jolly Ox. The terms of my employment were simple: "playing an original song will get you fired on the spot!" A few days after Townes bested me on the girlfriend front, I announced to the Jolly Ox crowd that I'd be ending the set with a song I'd just written called "You Can't Keep Me Here In Tennessee." As soon as the song ended, the bar manager came charging down the aisle leading to the small stage. A few steps behind him was a pleasant-looking fellow in a coat and tie. My boss hissed loud enough to be heard by the gentleman trailing him that I was indeed fired. "That's good news," said the stranger, "because *my* boss wants to record that song tomorrow." He also declared that his boss was prepared to offer me a job writing songs for his publishing company. The man's name was Harry Warner, and his boss was Jerry Reed.

When I showed up early the next morning at RCA's Studio A, Chet Atkins—the most famous musician, producer, and record executive in all of Nashville—was sitting alone at the recording console. "You write the tune we're recording today?" he asked politely. I must have nodded yes because the next thing I know I'm playing it for him. Twenty minutes later, I'm teaching the chord progression to session musicians I'd been reading about for years. In less than a week I'd gone from a tip-basket nobody to a hundred-dollar-a-week professional songwriter. It's only now that I realize I never thanked Townes and the free-loving, hippie girl for helping get the ball rolling.

You Can't Keep Me Here in Tennessee

By the time we left Kentucky all that was on my mind
Was the way I'd spent my trouble like a dime
When we got back to Nashville things were still the same
And my thoughts ran back to Texas, I hoped to ease the pain

Because you fall like a tree when you've been cut down
And you've been too long hacking away at me
It's a long old road I'm taking back to Texas
'Cause you can't keep me here in Tennessee

In all my looking at you it's funny, all the things I've never seen
The sun don't shine beside you, least wise it ain't ever shone on me

Because you fall like a tree when you've been cut down
And you've been too long hacking away at me
It's a long old road I'm taking back to Texas
'Cause you can't keep me here in Tennessee

My mind's been in a dungeon, a prisoner in your world of make believe
I'm begging for your pardon, I've served my time and now I'll take my leave

Cause you fall like a tree when you've been cut down
And you've been too long hacking away at me
It's a long old road I'm taking back to Texas
'Cause you can't keep me here in Tennessee

'73

Dan Reeder

Dan Reeder

Thomas Petillo

CHART TOPPERS

Song for the Life I Have Found

I don't drink as much as I ought to
Lately it just ain't my style
The hard times and heartaches I've lived through
Passed as quickly as a lost lover's smile

Somehow I learned how to listen
For a sound like the sun going down
In the magic that morning is bringing
There's a song for the life I have found
To keep my feet on the ground

The midsummer days ain't so heavy
They just flow like a breeze through your mind
And nothing appears in a hurry
To make up for some old lost time

Somehow I learned how to listen
For a sound like the sun going down
In the magic that morning is bringing
There's a song for the life I have found
To keep my feet on the ground

Somehow I learned how to listen
For a sound like the breeze dying down
In the magic that morning is bringing
There's a song for the friend I have found
To keep my feet on the ground

'73

Song for the life

Rodney Crowell

WJ

I dont drink as much as I used too
Lately thats just not my style
The hard times dont hurt like they used too
They pass quicker like when I was a child
Some how I learned how to listen
To a sound like the sun going down
In the majic the morning is bringing
Theres a song for the life I have found
The midsummer days sit so heavy
Dont they flow like the breeze all the time
When nothing appears in a hurry
To make up for some ones lost time.

—o—

73

Fools Thin Air

Rodney Crowell
Suzanna Clark

Theres a sweet dream on your pillow
Theres a sad song in your eye
Theres the sun shine behind the dark cloud
Up above you in fools thin air
She's an old friend she's a good friend
Hair of golden eyes of satin
She's a wont be long friend, until shes gone and
Leaves you hanging in fools thin air
Like a lion rules the jungle
Your just flying the fools thin air
That dont mean nothing when youve got something
That you believe in to get you there.

75

Voila, An American Dream

I beg your pardon, mama, what did you say?
My mind was drifting on a Martinique day
It's not that I'm not interested, you see
Augusta, Georgia, is just no place to be

Just think Jamaica in the moonlight
Sandy beaches, drinking rum every night
We've got no money, mama, but we can go
We'll split the difference, go to Coconut Grove

Keep on talking, mama, I like the sound
It goes so good with the rain falling down
I feel a tropical vacation this year
Could be the answer to this hillbilly beer

Just think Jamaica in the moonlight
Sandy beaches, drinking rum every night
We've got no money, mama, but we can go
We'll split the difference, go to Coconut Grove

Voila, an American dream
We can travel, girl, without any means
It's as easy as closing your eyes
And dream Jamaica is a big neon sign

Keep on talking, mama, I can hear
You voice it tickles down inside of my ear
I feel a tropical vacation this year
Might be the answer to this near beer down here

Voila, an American dream
We can travel, girl, without any means
It's as easy as closing your eyes
And dream Jamaica is a big neon sign

'74

Ashes By Now

This morning is Monday, where are you now?
Teasing my memory, teaching me how
To lay low when I don't want to

Love is elusive, this I know now
It's making me crazy, leaving me out in the open
When I don't want to lose you

Moments of pleasure never do last
Gone like a suitcase full of your past
Long gone and in a hurry

Baby, I can't go through this again
I don't need to go down more than I've already been
Just like a wildfire, you're running all over town
As much as you burn me, baby, I should be ashes by now

Second Street beggars alone in their life
Drunk on the sidewalk to hide from the night, like I am
They're just like I am

Baby, I can't go through this again
I don't need to go down more than I've already been
Just like a wildfire, you're running all over town
As much as you burn me, baby, I should be ashes by now
Just like a wildfire, you're running all over town
As much as you burn me, baby, I should be ashes by now

'74

(JAMAICA IN THE MOONLIGHT)

AN AMERICAN DREAM

Rodney Crowell

I Beg your Pardon Momma What Did you say
my mind was Drifting on a Martinique Day
Its Not that Im not Interested you See
Augusta Georgia Is Just No Place to Be

Just Think Jamaica In the moonlight
Sandy Beaches Drinkin Rum every Night
Weve Got No money momma But we can go
well split the Difference + Go to Cocanut Grove

Just Keep on talking momma I can Hear
your Voice It tickles Down Inside of my Ear
I feel A tropical Vacation this year → All This HillBilly Beer
Could Be the Answer to American Beer

Just Think Jamaica In the moonlight
Sandy Beaches Drinking Rum every Night
Weve Got No Money momma But we Can Go
Just split the Differece + go to Cocanut Grove

Voila ~~AHLA~~ An American Dream, we can travel Girl without any means
when Its as easy as Closing your Eyes
+ Dream Jamaica Is A Big Neon Sign

Keep on Taking momma I like the Sound
Its Going Good with the Rain falling Down

74

The Morning is monday where are you now
teasing my memory teaching me how
to Lay low when I dont want to

this I know now
Lovers a loser I found it out
+ it making me crazy leaving me out
in the open when I dont want to

Baby I cant go through this again
I dont need to go down more than I already been
~~and sat feel for myself~~

Like a wildfire your running all over town
As much as you burn me I should be Ashes by now.

Like the Blue Sky I know your out there somewher
(Like a whirlwind you turn my head all around)
Like a whirlpool it Im drowning in you.

The moments of Pleasure never do last
theyre gone like a suitcase full of the Past
Long gone and in a hurry

Second ~~st~~ beggars alone in they life
Drunk on the sidewalk to hide from the night
Like I am

Like a sad and ~~bad~~
~~When I see you take your never~~
In as much as you burn me I should be Ashes by Now
Like a wildfire your running all over town
~~Like a Rolling Stone~~
~~Like the Sun on the Beach~~ your belly burning I'm down
Baby ~~you got me sinking~~ I cant go through this again
I dont want to go down
more than Ive already been

(Skippers Blues)

Rodney Crowell

ASHES BY NOW

The Morning is Monday where are you now
Teasing my memory teaching me how
To Lay low when I dont want to
Lovers a loser this I know now
making me crazy leaving me out
in the open when I dont want to
The moments of Pleasure never do Last
theyre gone like a suitcase full of your Past
Long Gone and in a Hurry
Baby I cant go through this again
I dont need to go down more than Ive already been
Just like a wildfire your running all over town
As much as you burn me I should be Ashes by now
Second street Beggars alone in they life
Drunk on a sidewalk to hide from the night
Like I am theyre just like I am.

Mona

I can give you golden tinkling bells, to weave and dangle through your long black hair, I can give you magic satin slippers woven just to take you anywhere, I can give you all the love and tenderness a broken heart can spare, Mona take the love I give dont ask for love I gave away back there.

You could take the hand of any man and show him how to treat you, why do you look back into my dark and bitter past cant you see, Mona when you found me all I had was sad and broken dreams, Mona please be satisfied walking through tomorrow here with me

TILL I GAIN CONTROL AGAIN

I met Emmylou Harris in 1974 at the Childe Harold, one of the Washington DC's premier folk clubs, where she and the Angel Band were performing. Based on her reaction to the songs on the tape Skip Beckwith had delivered to his door, Brian Ahern offered me a deal that was nearly identical to Jerry Reed's, an investment that warranted he and I taking a trip from Toronto down to DC to see if Emmylou and I would hit it off. Introductions were made backstage after the show, as were plans to meet up the following evening at John and Fayssoux Starling's townhouse. I remember several Angel Band members turning up, but John Starling was nowhere to be seen. This disappointment didn't last long. Emmylou, Fayssoux, and I found a spot on the kitchen floor and started singing three-part harmony to every old song we could think of. Sometime before sunrise, I mentioned that I'd just written a song they might like to hear. Fayssoux claims she recorded my first ever performance of "Till I Gain Control Again" on some little device, which could very well be true because the next time our paths crossed in Austin's Armadillo World Headquarters, Emmylou was excited to tell me that, with Brian's help, she'd recorded a killer version of the song. There were many more covers to come, but only a few were anywhere close to hers.

One such performance came out of a 1977 Willie Nelson recording session that I traveled to Bogalusa, Louisiana, to play and sing on. The collaboration started in North Hollywood at the Palomino Club, California's premier honky-tonk, when the great Texas balladeer announced he wanted to do a Rodney Crowell song, and called me up on stage to sing a harmony part. I remember thinking as I headed to the bandstand, *This feels like being knighted by one of the masters!* At that moment I knew I'd found my rightful place in the world of songwriting, a feeling that has never changed.

Naturally, I was overjoyed to be singing harmony and playing a rather timid rhythm guitar on Willie's studio recording of "Till I Gain Control Again." Listening to the playback in the control room, I was convinced we'd cut a number-one record. Willie's inspired performance wasn't released until 2020. Back then he'd gone with a live version instead, which had left the door wide open for Crystal Gayle to take her beautiful rendition to the top of the charts in 1983.

Steve Schneider

Dan Reeder

Just like the sun over the mountian tops
you know I'll always come again
you know I love to spend my morning time
Like sunlight dancing on your skin
Ive never gone so wrong as for telling lies to you
what you've seen is what Ive been
There is nothing I could hide from you
You see me better than I can

Out on the road that lies before me now
There are some turns where I will spin
I'd only hoped that you can hold me now
Till I can gain control again

Like a light house you must stand alone
Land mark a sailors journeys end
No matter what seas Ive been sailing on
I'll always roll this way again.

Till I Gain Control Again

Just like the sun over the mountain tops
You know I'll always come again
You know I love to spend my morning time
Like sunlight dancing on your skin

I've never gone so wrong as for telling lies to you
What you've seen is what I've been
There is nothing I could hide from you
You see me better than I can

Out on the road that lies before me now
There are some turns where I will spin
I only hope that you can hold me now
Till I can gain control again

Like a lighthouse, you might stand alone
Landmark a sailor's journey's end
No matter what sea I've been sailing on
I'll always roll your way again

Out on the road that lies before me now
There are some turns where I will spin
I only hope that you can hold me now
Till I can gain control again
I only hope that you can hold me now
Till I can gain control again

'74

LEASH LAWS AND DOG RUSTLERS

In August of 1973, a little girl gave me a stray dog her parents wouldn't let her keep. Having recently read Tolkien's *The Hobbit*, and having been smitten by Bilbo Baggins, it's main character, I promptly christened the whiskery little mutt Bilbo, an insipid name I knew, but the little girl seemed pleased, and I figured a more dog-worthy one would occur to me eventually.

When "Bilbo" was maybe five-weeks-old, Jerry Jeff Walker blew into town, and the house Harlan White and I had rented on 19th Avenue became the site of a marathon song-swapping bash. For a day and a half, Nashville songwriters of every stripe dropped by to pay their respects to the man who wrote "Mister Bojangles" and, of course, to play him a new song or two. Which was fine with me. But as a strain of insomniacs and hangers-on kept filing through the door, I grew progressively more worried that my puppy stood a good chance of being petted to death. I was on the verge of making some kind of warning about that when the guest of honor freed him from some fool's grasp and declared there would be "no more man-handling of Banjo here." My correction—"It's *Bilbo*"—was ignored, and I let it go.

As the party picked up speed, Jerry Jeff and Guy Clark took turns claiming this or that new song a keeper, the former all-the-while making a big show of cradling the little furball in the crook of his arm. I didn't much care for the contented look on their faces. Not until I separated the new best friends long enough to stash Bilbo in his laundry-lined cardboard box I'd rigged up for his bed, was I finally able to relax and join the festivities.

Around six in the morning, after the second night of gonzo merriment, I could go no further, and left our guest of honor and the last few stragglers to find their own way out. I'd been asleep for maybe an hour when the phone rang and Dave Loggins alerted me that Jerry Jeff had stolen my dog and was headed for the airport. In less than a minute—having crashed out in my street clothes—I hopped into my '53 Dodge panel truck and sped off. Those being the carefree days before airport security, slamming on the brakes beside the departure curb barely raised an eyebrow. Nor did leaving the motor running and sprinting to the gate where commuters were starting to board the plane.

The first thing I noticed were the custom-tooled saddlebags draped over the dog rustler's shoulder.

"What's in those saddlebags, Jerry Jeff?"

"Boots," he said, innocence radiating behind his crinkly grin.

"Let's see 'em."

"Come on out, Banjo," he cooed into Bilbo's muzzle, and was rewarded with a round of love licks that made me jealous. Forking over my puppy, he muttered, "At least you could call him by his name."

When the first leg of the Emmylou Harris and the Hot Band tour of 1975 ended in July, I flew home to Austin to check on Banjo. Though Muffin and I had called it quits, she was the only person I trusted to look after my dog. And while he greeted me with due affection, it was obvious that Banjo had formed a deeper bond with my ex-girlfriend. More out of pity than guilt, Muffin invited me to stay—in the apartment were I was paying rent—until the second leg kicked in. And for five restful days, all was forgiven.

In early August I found a small bungalow less than three blocks from the ocean in Hermosa Beach, California. In September, Muffin called to tell me she was pregnant and intended to have the child whether or not I wanted to be involved. When I asked if the baby was mine she said it was; and with that the matter was settled. She and Banjo would join me in California, and soon I would be a father. We were married by a justice of the peace on October 16th, and Banjo was the best man.

By the spring of '76 I'd ignored forty-seven Hermosa Beach leash law violations. I tried explaining to the dog catcher that Banjo was far too smart to be tethered to any human, and if they could understand that I was actually *his* pet, they'd know it wasn't my place to hinder his roaming. They looked at me as if I'd just crawled out of a spaceship. One mid-morning in April, I was sitting at my makeshift desk trying to coax a song out of a boogie-woogie riff that was stuck in my head when three Hermosa Beach patrolmen knocked on the screen door. I was read my rights and arrested for the unpaid violations. Handcuffed, I got a clear picture of how the song should go. I called out to my eight-and-a-half-months-pregnant wife from inside the squad car: "Take your time getting me out, I want to work on the song." Being a good sport, and as guilty as I was of not paying the fines, Muffin granted me four hours of jail-time, during which I finalized the lyrical structure for "I Ain't Living Long Like This," one of my more durable compositions. Only later did it occur to me that I should've given Banjo and Muffin co-writing credits.

Banjo died of prostate cancer on the day John Lennon was murdered in 1980. So I wept long and hard twice over. Not long ago, a very old and wizened Banjo visited me in a dream. I was given to understand that he was still *my* dog, and would be forever.

I Ain't Living Long Like This

I looked for trouble and I found it, son
Straight down the barrel of a lawman's gun
I'd try to run but I don't think I can
You make one move and you're a dead man, friend

I ain't living long like this, I can't live at all like this, can I, baby?
He slipped the handcuffs on behind my back
And left me freezing on a steel-rail rack
They've got 'em all in the jailhouse, baby
I ain't living long like this

Grew up in Houston off of Wayside Drive
Son of a carhop in some all-night dive
Dad drove a stock car to an early death
All I remember was a drunk man's breath

I ain't living long like this, I can't live at all like this, can I, baby?
You know the story how the wheel goes 'round
Don't let 'em take you to the man downtown
I can't sleep at all in the jailhouse, baby
I ain't living long like this
I can't live at all like this, can I, baby?

I live for Angel, she's a roadhouse queen
Makes Texas Ruby look like Sandra Dee
I want to love her but I don't know how
Down at the bottom of the jailhouse now

I ain't living long like this, I can't live at all like this, can I, baby?
You know the song about the "Jailhouse Rock"
Go on and do it but just don't get caught
They've got 'em all in the jailhouse, baby
I ain't living long like this
I can't live at all like this, can I, baby?

'76

Leaving Louisiana in the Broad Daylight

Mary took to running with a traveling man
Left her mama crying with her head in her hands
Such a sad case, so broken hearted
She'd say, Mama, gotta go, I've got to get out of here
I've gotta get out of town, I'm tired of hanging around
I've gotta roll on between the ditches
It's just an ordinary story 'bout the way things go
'Round and around nobody knows but the highway rolls on forever
That old highway goes on forever

She never would've done it if she hadn't got drunk
If she hadn't started running with a traveling man
If she hadn't started taking those crazy chances
She said daughter, let me tell you 'bout the traveling kind
Everywhere he's going, such a very short time
He'll be long gone before you know it
He'll be long gone before you know it

She says Never have I known it when it felt so good
Never have I knew it when I knew I could
Never have I done it when it looked so right
Leaving Louisiana in the broad daylight

This is down in the swampland where anything goes
It's alligator bait, and the bars don't close
It's the real thing down in Louisiana
Did you ever see a Cajun when he really got mad?
When he's really got trouble like a daughter gone bad?
It gets real hot down in Louisiana
So now the stranger better move it or he's gonna get killed
He's gonna have to get it or a shotgun will
This ain't no time for lengthy speeches
It ain't no time for lengthy speeches

She says Never have I known it when it felt so good
Never have I knew it when I knew I could
Never have I done it when it looked so right
Leaving Louisiana in the broad daylight

Never have I known it when it felt so good
Never have I knew it when I knew I could
Never have I done it when it looked so right
Leaving Louisiana in the broad daylight

It's just an ordinary story 'bout the way things go
'Round and around nobody knows
But the highway goes on forever
That ole highway goes on forever

Rodney Crowell & Donivan Cowart
1976

(thanks to Mary Kay Place)

LEAVING LOUSIANA IN THE BROAD DAYLIGHT

Rodney Crowell & Donivan Cowart

MARY TOOK to Running with A TRAVELIN MAN
Left HER momma CRYING with her HEAD IN HER HAND
Such A SAD CASE SO BROKEN HEARTED
SHE SAY MOMMA I GOT to GO I GOT to GET OUTA HERE
I GOT to GET out of TOWN IM TIRED of HANGING AROUND
I GOT to Roll ON BETWEEN the Ditches
Its JUST AN ORDINARY story Bout the way thINGS GOES
ROUND AND AROUND NOBODY KNOWS But the HIGHWAY
Rolls ON forever, That ol HIGHWAY GOES ON FOREVER
LORD she NEVER would've DONE it IF she HADN'T GOT DRUNK
IF she HADN'T STARTED Running with A TRAVELIN MAN
IF she HADN'T STARTED TAKING those CRAZY CHANCES
she say DAUGHTER Let me tell you Bout the TRAVELIN KIND
EVERYWHERE he's going such A VERY SHORT TIME
He'll Be LONG GONE BEFORE you know it, He'll Be
LONG GONE BEFORE you know it

CHORUS
She SAY NEVER HAVE I KNOWN It when It Felt so
GOOD, NEVER HAVE I KNEW when I Knew I COULD
NEVER HAVE I DONE It when It Looked so RIGHT
LEAVING LOUSIANA IN the BROAD DAYLIGHT

This IS DOWN IN the SWAMP LAND ANYthING GOES
Its Alligator Bait AND the BARS DONT Close
Its The REAL THING DOWN IN LOUSIANA
DID you EVER SEE A CAJUN when He Really Got MAD
when He Really Got TROUBLE Like A DAUGHTER GONE BAD
IT GETS REAL HOT DOWN IN LOUSIANA
Now the STRANGER Better move IT OR He's Gonna Get Kill
Hes Gonna Have to Get It or A Shot Gun Will
This Aint NO TIME FOR Lengthy SPEECHES, IT AINT NO
TIME FOR Lengthy SPEECHES

Even Cowgirls Get the Blues (For Emylou + Tom Robbins) Rodney Crowell

Shes A Rounder I can tell you that
She can sing em all night too
She'll raise hell about the sleep she lost
But even cowgirls get the blues
Especially cowgirls theyre the gypsy kind
+ need their reigns laid on em loose
She lived to see the world turned upside down
Hitching rides out of the blue
But even cowgirls get the blues sometimes
Bound to dont know what to do sometimes
Get this feeling ~~like~~ shes too far gone
the only way she's ever been
Lonely nights are what are on the road
Motel ceilings stare you down
Must be safer ways to pay your dues
But even cowgirls get the blues.
(~~Get~~ this feeling like the Restless Wind, the only way she's ever been)

—o—

A Fool Such As I

Pardon me if im sentimental when we say goodbye
Dont be angry with me should I cry
Im a fool but I love you dear until the day I die
Now + then theres a fool such as I, Now + then theres a fool
such as I am over you. You taught me how to love and now
you say that we are through
Im a fool but I love you dear until the day I die
Now + then theres a fool such as I.

—o—

Even Cowgirls Get the Blues

She's a rounder, I can tell you that
She can sing 'em all night too
She'll raise hell about the sleep she lost
Even cowgirls get the blues

Especially cowgirls, they're the gypsy kind
And need their reins laid on 'em loose
She's lived to see the world turned upside down
Hitching rides out of the blue

Even cowgirls get the blues sometimes
Bound to don't know what to do sometimes
Get this feeling like she's too far gone
The only way she's ever been

Lonely nights are out there on the road
A motel ceiling stares you down
There must be safer ways to pay your dues
Even cowgirls get the blues

Even cowgirls get the blues sometimes
Bound to don't know what to do sometimes
Get this feeling like she's too far gone
The only way she's ever been

Even cowgirls get the blues sometimes
Bound to don't know what to do sometimes
Get this feeling like the restless wind
The only way she's ever been

'77

No Memories Hanging Around

You don't want no more heartaches
I don't want no teardrops
What else is left to talk about?
I ain't yours, you ain't mine
Songs don't fit and the words don't rhyme
Old memories keep standing in the way

> I lost her, you lost him
> Two old hearts just won't love again
> They don't need no memories hanging 'round

Since she's gone it don't feel right
I'm better off left alone at night
I ain't faking feeling far away
The days just come and disappear
You can't talk and I can't hear
It makes no difference anyway

> I lost her, you lost him
> Two old hearts just won't love again
> They don't need no memories hanging 'round

> I want her, you need him
> Two old fires just won't burn again
> They don't need no memories hanging 'round

'78

There Ain't No Money in the Ones That You Really Love

Every day now I hear people say
My ship is sailing, could be any day
Any day now I might not feel so blue
My baby tells me stop and look around
If you ain't careful, boy, you're trouble bound
Run home for cover and you might not find none there

She says there ain't no money in this running around
And you can't make money staying at home
And there ain't no future in the way that you feel today

There ain't no money, there ain't no money
There ain't no money in the ones that you really love

I try to tell it to 'em straight and true
No love for money tells you what to do
You're born to ramble and that's what I was too
Just breaking even, even if I lose
Old lucky seven got a hold on you
I've got your number, baby, any way you move

There ain't no money, that's for sure
There ain't no money behind no door
And there ain't no trouble that a poor boy won't go through

There ain't no money, there ain't no money
There ain't no money in the ones that you really love

'78

AINT NO MONEY

EVERY DAY I HEAR PEOPLE SAY
MY SHIP IS SAILING COULD BE ANY DAY
ANY DAY NOW (MIGHT NOT BE SO BLUE)
JUST DONT EVER COME

? ~~[illegible]~~ AHEAD
?
?

BUT THERE AINT NO MONEY IN THE RUNNIN AROUND
CANT MAKE MONEY IN STAYIN AT HOME
+ THERE AINT NO FUTURE IN THE WAY THAT
WE FEEL TODAY
CAUSE THERE AINT NO MONEY IN THE LIFE WE LIVE
?
NO THERE AINT NO MONEY IN THE ONES THAT
YOU REALLY LOVE
NO THERE AINT NO MONEY BABY THERE AINT NO MONEY
NO THERE AINT NO MONEY IN THE ONES THAT
YOU REALLY LOVE

BABY TELL ME STOP + LOOK AROUND
I DONT HEAR THE SOUND
BUT I DONT LISTEN CAUSE IM TROUBLE BOUND
HURRY UP + WAIT FOR THE TIME TO COME
OF MY OWN STEPS A WALKIN

IF YOU AINT CAREFULL YOU'LL BE TROUBLE BOUND
RUN HOME FOR COVER + YOU MIGHT NOT
FIND ME THERE

EVERY DAY NOW I HEAR PEOPLE SAY
MY SHIP IS SAILING COULD BE ANY DAY
ANY DAY NOW MIGHT NOT FEEL SO BLUE
MY BABY TELLS ME STOP + LOOK AROUND
IF YOU AINT CAREFUL BOY YOUR TROUBLE BOUND
RUN HOME FOR COVER + YOU MIGHT NOT FIND ME
THERE
+ THERE AINT NO MONEY IN THE RUNNING AROUND
YOU CANT MAKE MONEY STAYIN AT HOME
+ THERE AINT NO FUTURE IN THE WAY
THAT IT FEELS TODAY
LORD THERE AINT NO MONEY BABY THERE AINT NO
MONEY
BABY THERE AINT NO MONEY IN THE ONES
THAT YOU REALLY LOVE

THERE AINT NO TROUBLE LIKE YOU MUST GO THROUGH
~~BABY ALL THE TROUBLE~~ STRAIT + TRUE
~~[illegible]~~ ~~THROUGH + TH~~
I TRY TO TELL EM BABY ~~BUT I CAN~~ I CAN COME NEAR TO YOU
~~I DONT NEED IT~~ NO LOVE NO MORE ~~IT DONT FIT MY PL~~
YOU LOVE TO RAMBLE BABY THATS WHAT
I LOVE TOO
~~JUST~~ BREAKIN EVEN EVEN IF I LOSE
~~MY NIGHTS ARE~~
~~I GOT YOUR~~ NUM~~BERS ANY WAY~~ YOU DO
COME OUT ON TOP OF EVERYONE YOU CHOSES
I GOT YOUR NUMBER BABY ANY WAY YOU MOVE
THERE AINT NO MONEY BABY THATS FOR SURE
THERE AINT NO MONEY BEHIND NO DOORS
THERE AINT NO TROUBLE
THAT A HEARTACHE MUST GO THROUGH

SHAME ON ME

I was staring at the muted TV and strumming a G-major to E-minor chord pattern when I began attaching mumbling sounds to an emerging melody. This went on until a B-flat climbing back up to the G triggered the phrase "Oh, blame it on midnight, ooh, shame on the moon." I knew then that a song was forming in the nether regions of my subconscious. Verses one and two came quickly. Both needed revisions, but for the moment I let them stand in favor of capturing a third verse while the song was still making itself known to me. Serious editing would come later. The gist of a last stanza was beginning to take shape when news of the Jim Jones mass suicide in Guyana flashed across the television screen, and whatever access I'd had to the song's best intentions instantly disappeared. It was as if I'd been yanked out a dream and dumped into some filmic version of a hellish trance. This was the last time I ever allowed a TV within sight of where I'm attempting to coax a song out of hiding.

Although dissatisfied with the last verse of "Shame on the Moon," I went ahead and recorded a version that Bob Seger got hold of and turned into the most successful cover of anything I've ever written. As much as I appreciated the windfall, I was even more grateful that Bob's performance was so definitively superior to mine that I could delete the song from my live performance repertoire. Nevertheless, I spent nearly four decades trying to revise the third verse with nothing to show for my efforts. In 2018, it was suggested that I do an all-acoustic album of some of my more recognizable tunes. Only then did it dawn on me that instead of trying to conjure up a new and improved third verse to something thirty-nine years old, I might have better luck reimagining all three verses. Thus was born "Shame on the Moon Redux." A few trusted friends are divided on whether the couplets that survived the Jones massacre serve the song's ethereal purpose more effectively than the painstakingly revised narrative. Who can say which is right? Although I think the rewritten version is technically superior to the original, it might not be better. For personal reasons, I'm including three sets of lyrics in this retrospective.

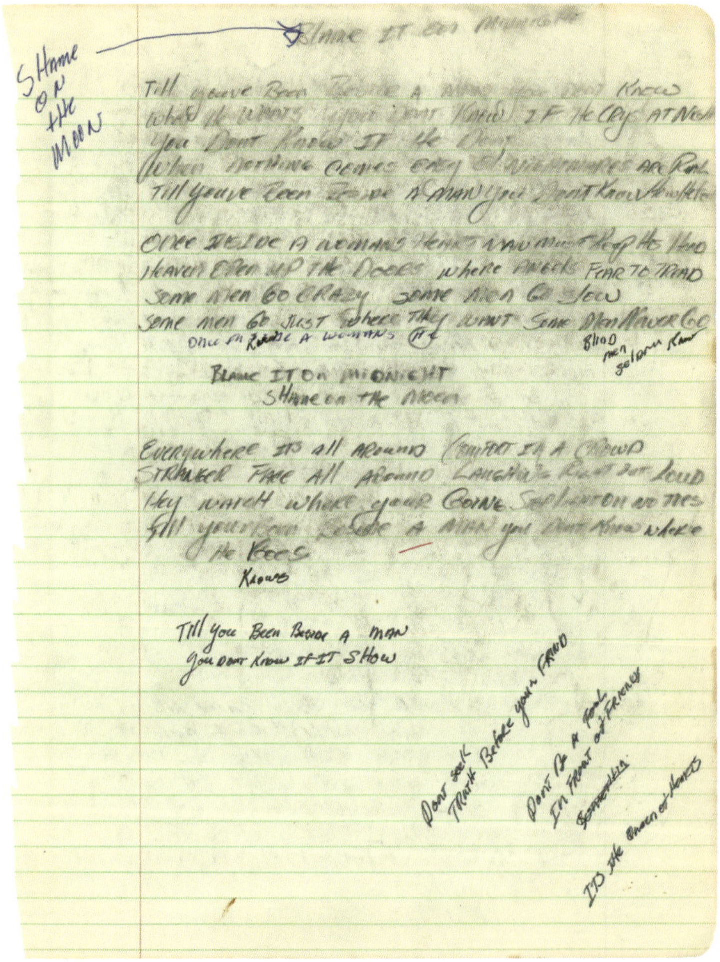

Jennifer Tzar

Shame on the Moon

Till you've been beside a man you don't know what he wants
You don't know if he cries at night, you don't know if he don't
When nothing comes easy old nightmares are real
Till you've been beside a man you don't know how he feels

Once inside a woman's heart, a man must keep his head
Heaven opens up the door where angels fear to tread
Some men go crazy, some men go slow
Some men go just where they want, some men never go

Oh, blame it on midnight
Ooh, shame on the moon

Everywhere is all around, comfort in a crowd
Strangers' faces all about, laughing right out loud
Hey, watch where you're going, step light on your toes
Until you've been beside a man you don't know who he knows

Oh, blame it on midnight
Ooh, shame on the moon

Oh, blame it on midnight
Ooh, shame on the moon

1979

R. Crowell

Shame on the Moon

Till you've been beside a man you don't know what he wants
You don't know if he cries at night you don't know if he don't
When nothing comes easy old nightmares are real
Till you've been beside a man you don't know how he feels

Once inside a woman's heart a man must keep his head
Heaven opened up the door where angels fear to tread
Some men go crazy some men go slow
Some men go just where they want
Some men never go
ooo Blame it on midnight
oh Shame on the moon

Every where its all around comfort in a crowd
Strangers faces all around laughing right out loud
Hey watch where your going step light on your toes
Till you've been beside a man you don't know what he knows
oh Blame it on midnight
ooo Shame on the moon

-0-

Shame on the Moon Redux

It wasn't all that long ago that I could really drink 'em down
Three days up and running wild and never touch the ground
If tall, dark and handsome is not what I am
You've either not noticed or you don't give a damn
I've heard it said a thousand times, "to thine on self be true"
But it's not for lack of trying that this is something I can't do
So what can I tell you that you don't already know?
The chinks in my armor are starting to show

Oh, blame it on midnight
Ooh, shame on the moon

Once inside a woman's heart, a man must keep his head
Heaven opens up the doors where angels fear to tread
The sidewalks are empty, I feel like a ghost
A kindhearted stranger now is what I need most

Oh, blame it on midnight
Ooh, shame on the moon

2018

You could say I'm an honest man
you could say I'm a rake
to really see the best in me
Requires a second take

…the Moon Redux

Though you could say that I'm not

…is I'm an honest man it's seldom that I lie
…on occasion I've been known to falsify
…tell you, that you don't already know
…in my armor are starting to show

…a woman's heart a man… …eep his head
…ns up the doors where… …ar to tread"
…in my twenties and hung… …ise
…like crazy when I wrote… …hat phrase

…on midnight
…on the moon

…s are empty now and I… …a ghost
…stranger is what I…
…and handsome is not wh…
…she'll not notice or won't give a damn

…on midnight
…on the moon

…on midnight
…on the moon

It's not like I'm a Gentleman
Nor am I just a Rake
To see the very best in me
Requires a Second Take

Shame on the Moon

Till you've been beside a man you don't know what he wants
You don't know if he cries at night, you don't know if he don't
When nothing comes easy, old nightmares are real
Till you've been beside a man you don't know how he feels

Once inside a woman's heart, a man must keep his head
Heaven opens up the door where angels fear to tread
Some men go crazy, some men go slow
Some men know just what they want, some men never know

Oh, blame it on midnight
Ooh, shame on the moon

I've heard it said a thousand times, "To thine own self be true"
And it's not for lack of trying, this is something I can't do
The sidewalks are empty, I feel like a ghost
And a kindhearted stranger is what I need most

Oh, blame it on midnight
Ooh, shame on the moon
Oh, blame it on midnight
Ooh, shame on the moon

2022

After All This Time

There were trains and we outrun 'em
There were songs and we outsung 'em
There were brighter days never ending

There was time and we were burning
There were rhymes and we were learning
There was all the love two hearts could hold

After all this time you're always on my mind
I could never let it end 'cause my heart takes so long to mend
The dream that keeps your hopes alive, the lonely nights you hold inside
And after all this time you're always on my mind, I still want you

There was rain that we outlasted
There was pain but we got past it
There were last goodbyes still left unspoken

There were ways I should have thrilled you
There were days when I could have killed you
You're the only woman I ever wanted that much

And after all this time you're always on my mind
Hey, I could never let you go, a broken heart that heals so slow
Could never beat for someone new while you're alive and I am too
And after all this time you're always on my mind, I still miss you

And I could never let it end 'cause my heart takes so long to mend
The dream that keeps your hopes alive, the lonely nights you hold inside
And after all this time you're always on my mind, I still want you
Hey, after all this time you're always on my mind, I still love you

'78-'85

After All this Time

The Dreams that Keep
your Hopes Alive
Are Lonely Nights
I Hold Inside

There was Trains + we OutRun Em
There were Songs + we out sung Em
There were Brighter Days Never Ending
There was Time + we was Burnin
There was Rhymes + we was Learnin
There was All of the Love Two Hearts Could Hold
After All this time youre always on my mind
I could never let ~~it~~ END cause my Heart takes so long to mend
These lonely nights I Hold Inside
the A Dream that Keeps your Hopes Alive all thats
youre ~~still~~ on my mind
+ After all this time youre always on my mind
I still Love you

These were Days
There were Times when we were younger
so alive + Full of Hunger
~~Tell~~ when Tear drops fell on Salty Kisses

I still want you
I still Need you

I could never let you Go
A Broken Heart that heals so slow
~~you~~ could never Beat for someone new
while youre alive + I Am to
After All ~~this~~ time its still Hard but it But I dont know
I still want you

I Couldn't Leave You If I Tried

The sun is coming up and I'm just goin' down
Everywhere I look the world keeps turnin' 'round
Though I said I never would be satisfied
Baby, I lied, I couldn't leave you if I tried

Sometimes I get lost out on this sad old town
And every bridge I cross just turns me upside down
And every stumbling step I take back to your side
It hurts my pride, I couldn't leave you if I tried

Well, I could not walk away no matter what I say
I won't be leaving, believe it or don't, you're all that I want

Tears may fall but after all is said and done
Darlin' please believe, me you're the only one
And I'll admit mistakes I've made me realize
Baby, I lied, I couldn't leave you if I tried

I won't be leaving you no matter what I do
I'm gonna see it through 'til the end and do it again

Years may come and friends may go but that's okay
Darlin' you're the only one I need to stay
I know I said I never would be satisfied
Baby, I lied, I couldn't leave you if I tried
I couldn't leave you if I tried

'86

2) I Couldn't Leave You If I Tried

(Rodney Crowell)

~~Harmony Vocal~~ Vince Gill

Twin Fiddles: Glen Duncan

With his pockets full of earned treasures, the Appalachian "dead baby" songs he learned from his Gran[illegible], the honky tonk classics (and semi classics) he played each [illegible] end with his dad, his well thumbed texts, Mr Berry, [illegible] Dylan and Mr. Williams chief among them, and of course [illegible] years and counting of his own songs, Rodney's made a [illegible] record.

He tells me this new record (Diamonds + Dirt) is a return to his rodeo dance band days back in Texas. He's also told me he "never did manage to stay on a bull for eight damned seconds. "If I did my life might be totally [illegible]. I'm pleased with the way things turned out. I suspect he is too

Jeff Nesin

FROM THE DESK OF... Rodney

The Sun is coming up + I'm just going down

Must admit how much it hurts

~~Everywhere~~ I look around

Though I said you'd never keep me satisfied / No one could never keep me

Babe I lied

I couldn't leave you if I tried

Rain tears may fall but after all is said + done

Darlin please believe me you're the only one

Though I said no one could keep me mystified

Babe I lied

I couldn't leave you if I tried

FROM THE DESK OF... Rodney

Sometimes I get lost out on the midnight road

Every bridge I cross just turns me down

Darlin I get lost out on the road

Every bridge I cross just turns me [illegible]

Though I said I never would be satisfied

Babe I lied I couldn't leave you if I tried

The Sun is coming up + I'm just going down

Everywhere I look ~~[illegible]~~ I see the [illegible]

Every stumblin step I take [illegible]

[illegible] your side

It's Such a Small World

Fancy meeting you here tonight
It's such a small world
New York ain't my town
I don't come around but once in a while

This is such a surprise to see you
Girl, you're looking so good
It's been a long time since you've crossed my mind
It's such a small world

Just one night on the town
I came looking around for something to do

Just a change of my plans on leaving
And I stay around
And I run into you, which just goes to prove
It's such a small world

It's such a small world, I've lived alone for awhile
It's such a small world, I still keep my clothes in a pile

You and me will always be
Just looking for something that's already happened
Years go by but you and I don't have to look beyond today

Maybe just for tonight we can turn out the light
Lay your heart on the line, let go of your mind
You know just what to say, you know just what to do
You still look like the day when I first met you

I'll be gone once again come morning
Like I've always done
But to see you tonight makes everything right
It's such a small world
Right here you stand as if it was planned
It's such a small world

'86

CAN/ RIGHT THERE YOU STAND
AS IF IT WERE PLANNED
ITS SUCH A SMALL WORLD

FANCY MEETING YOU HERE + TONIGHT

ITS SUCH A SMALL WORLD
NEW YORK AINT MY TOWN I DONT
COME AROUND BUT ONCE IN A WHILE
THAT IS SUCH A SURPRISE TO SEE YOU
+ YOUR LOOKIN SO GOOD
ITS BEEN A LONG TIME SINCE YOU CROSSED MY MIND
ITS SUCH A SMALL WORLD
JUST ONE NIGHT ON THE TOWN
IM JUST LOOKIN AROUND
FOR SOMETHING TO DO
JUST A CHANGE OF MY PLANS ON LEAVIN
+ I STAYED AROUND
+ RUN INTO YOU
WHICH JUST GOES TO PROVE
ITS SUCH A SMALL WORLD
ITS SUCH A SMALL WORLD
(IVE LIVED ALONE FOR A WHILE)
ITS SUCH A SMALL WORLD

IVE KIND

SEEMS LIKE IVE GONE
OUT OF STYLE
I JUST

IVE FOUND MY OWN KIND OF STYLE)

IVE GOT NOTHING TO LOOSE BUT OL MEMORIES OF YOU
WHEN YOU WERE JUST YOUNG

IM AMAZED AT THE WAY
YOU STILL LOOK LIKE THE DAY
WHEN I FIRST MET YOU

ILL BE GONE ONCE
AGAIN COME MORNIN
LIKE IVE ALWAYS DONE

+ TO SEE YOU
TONIGHT
MAKES
EVERYTHING
RIGHT

~~YOUR A MEMORY TO LAST FOREVER~~
TO SEE YOU TONIGHT &
MAKES EVERYTHING
RIGHT
ITS SUCH A
SMALL
WORLD

SOME TIMES
I LONG
FOR YOUR
STYLE

She's Crazy for Leaving

The bus pulled away in a roaring black cloud
I stood in the road and, honey, I hollered right out loud

"Hey darling, I love you, hey bus driver, whoa"
But you can't stop a woman when she's out of control

She's crazy for leaving, I told her so
And the boys at the bus stop just said, "man, let her go!"
She's crazy for leaving, I told her so
But you can't stop a woman when she's out of control

So I punched out my truck on a telephone pole
She never looked back, she just said, "go, driver, go!"
I know I could've caught her but I ran out of luck
She was long on to Lufkin by the time they cut me out of my truck

She's crazy for leaving, I told her so
And the boys at the bus stop just said, "man, let her go!"
She's crazy for leaving, I told her so.
But you can't stop a woman when she's out of control

So I kicked and I cussed that old East Texas road
I throw'd rocks at my truck, which had busted my nose
Add insult to injury, and what do you get?
A bus stop of honkys that don't ever forget

She's crazy for leaving, I told her so
And the bus depot lady just said, "hon, let her go!"
She's crazy for leaving, I told her so
But you can't stop a woman when she's out of control
No, you can't stop a woman when she's out of control

Guy Clark & Rodney Crowell
'80

She's Crazy for Leavin

G. Clark
&
R. Crowell

Oh the bus pulled away in a roaring black cloud
I stood in the road honey I hollered right out loud
Hey darlin I love you hey bus driver whoa
But you cant stop a woman when she's out of control
She's crazy for leavin son I told her so
& the boys at the bus stop just said man let her go
She's crazy for leavin son I told her so
But you cant stop a woman who is out of control
So I pancaked out my truck on a telephone pole
Lord she never looked back she just said go driver go
I know I could have stopped her but I ran out of luck
She was long gone to Lufkin b'time the got me outta the truck
She's crazy for leavin I told her so
& the boys at the bus stop just said fool let her go
She's crazy for leavin son I told her so
But you cant stop a woman when she's out of control
So I kicked and I cussed that ol East Texas road
Throwed rocks at my truck which had busted my nose
Ad insult to injury & what do you get
A bus stop full of honkeys that dont ever forget
She's crazy for leavin son I told her so
& the bus depot lady just said hon I dont know
She's crazy for leavin son I told her so
But you cant stop a woman who is out of control

-0-

"80"

Dan Reeder

Many a Long and Lonesome Highway

Yes, I had a woman love me, I gave her what there was there of me
And it was good as it could be
Then I heard a wild world calling, I saw a lone star falling
I caught a song and set it free

Many a long and lonesome highway lies before us as we go
And in the end I'll do it my way, look for me where the four winds blow

I believe in love and danger, I believe the truth is stranger
I believe that fear is much too strong
I believe the best will find me when I leave the rest behind me
Out on the highway I'm my own

Many a long and lonesome highway lies before us as we go
In the end I'll do it my way, look for me where the four winds blow

Every night's a new beginning, every day the world keeps spinning
Sometimes it's hard to stand upon, I know
To the east the moon comes showing, to the west there's storm clouds growing
Though by myself, I'm not alone no more

My father, on his death bed told me, "there's nothing left to hold me"
Though I was there, he died alone
It's gonna take a fast train leaving to shake my world of grieving
I guess I'll go until it's gone

Many a long and lonesome highway lies before us as we go
And in the end I'll do it my way, look for me where the four winds blow
And many a long and lonesome highway lies before us as we go
In the end I'll do it my way, look for me where the four winds blow

RC & Will Jennings
'88

If Looks Could Kill

If today weren't just like any day, perhaps I'd try
To shed this worn out skin so thick and learn to fly
But I came home to face your ice and steel
If looks could kill I would be gone today

There's a fire that's burning in your eyes, not in your heart
And I can fan the flames but I can't make a spark
And I don't like the way I make you feel
If looks could kill I would be long since gone

If looks could kill then I'd be pushing up your daisies
If looks could kill then I would not be going crazy

There's a stool that I've been glued to for so many nights
And a bar to pour my heart out on and make it right
And I don't have to tell myself it's real
If looks could kill my heart would beat no more

And if looks could kill then I'd be deep in peaceful slumber
If looks could kill then I would not be going under

There's a gun out in the hallway covered up in rust
That works well enough to turn this heartache into dust
So, go on and let your lawyer make a deal
If looks could kill, if looks could kill I would be long since gone

'88

A buddy of mine asked me to write some words for his next album. He also said don't write about him or the songs. I spent the past week trying to do this because he's my pal and decided he wants a few words about LIFE! At first I thought "WHAT IS LIFE"? My immediate answer was LIFE is MUSIC! But then again we can't eat music even though it can eat us. So maybe then LIFE is LOVE! But it's hard to think about LOVE when your hungry or broke or have the flu or no one likes your MUSIC. So maybe LIFE is a CIRCLE, but if it is then all the lazy people like me would just stand still and wait for everyone to come back around. So I finally decided LIFE is FRIENDSHIP, and that's why I agreed to try to do something I didn't understand! FRIENDSHIP! This we give to each other in a steady warm trusting fashion and when LOVE and CIRCLES and MUSIC let us down, FRIENDS help us survive and come back to LIFE.

your FRIEND,

Harlan Howard

HARLAN HOWARD SONGS
1625 Otter Creek Road • Nashville, Tennessee 37215 • (615) 373-4080

Somewhere Tonight

Somewhere tonight he's a live wire
He's got his sights on someone new
Somewhere tonight he's a high flyer
And I'm so lonesome I don't know what to do

I bet he's out there shinin' like a diamond, don't you know
Turnin' heads, breakin' hearts and puttin' on a show
Rollin' like a summer storm, driftin' with the wind
And I just wish he'd blow my way again

Somewhere tonight he's a live wire
He's got his sights on someone new
Somewhere tonight he's a high flyer
And I'm so lonesome I don't know what to do

I've read that goodbye letter at least a thousand times
He said I was the only one who almost changed his mind
But better homes and garden parties, they weren't his cup of tea
Somewhere tonight he's runnin' wild and free

Somewhere tonight he's a live wire
He's got his sights on someone new
Somewhere tonight he's a high flyer
And I'm so lonesome I don't know what to do
And I'm so lonesome I don't know what to do

RC & Harlan Howard
'86

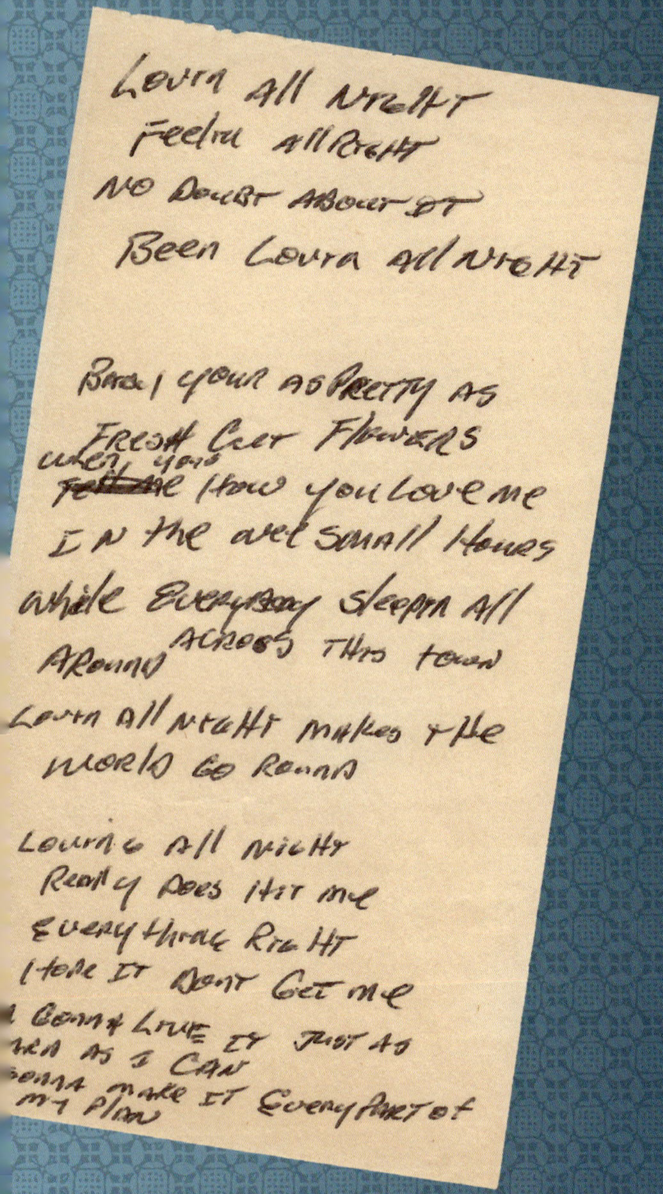
Lovin All Night
Feelin All Right
No Doubt About It
Been Lovin All Night

Baby your as pretty as
Fresh Cut Flowers
~~tell me~~ when you How you Love me
In the wee small Hours
while Everybody sleepin All
Around Across this town
Lovin All Night makes the
world go Round

Lovin All Night
Really does hit me
Everything Right
Hope It Dont Get me
I Gonna Live It Just As
long As I Can
Gonna make It Every Part of
my Plan

Loving All Night

Baby, pull the covers back over my head
I don't want to get up out of this bed
I don't want to drag it on off to work
That big boss man is really a jerk

We've been lovin' all night, just about thrilled me
Everything right, hope it don't kill me
I'm gonna live it just as long as I can
I'm gonna make it every part of my plan
Lovin' all night, hangin' on tight
No doubt about it, been lovin' all night, yeah

Baby, you're as pretty as a fresh cut flower
And when you show me how you love me in the wee small hours
While everybody's sleeping on around this town
Lovin' all night makes the world go 'round

We've been lovin' all night, just about sends me
Everything right, hope it don't bend me
I'm gonna live it just as long as I can
I'm gonna make it every part of my plan
Lovin' all night, hangin' on tight
No doubt about it, been lovin' all night, yeah

Ain't no use talkin' when you're lookin' so fine
When you're movin' your body up close to mine
We've been rockin' with a rhythm of a beat our own
Baby, I'm gonna love you 'til the cows come home

We've been lovin' all night, just about hit me
Everything right, hope it don't get me
I'm gonna live it just as long as I can
I'm gonna make it every part of my plan
Lovin' all night, feeling all right
No doubt about it, been lovin' all night
We've been lovin' all night, hanging on tight
No doubt about it, been lovin' all night

'90

What Kind of Love

I'll give you the best I can give you, baby, that's all I can give
We'll live it the best we can live it, baby, as long as we live

What kind of love never turns you down
What kind of love lifts you off the ground, turns your life around

What kind of love makes you go out in the wind and the driving rain
What kind of love runs through your heart with a pleasure so close to pain
What kind of love, only this love that I have

I'll show you the best I can show you, baby, that's all I can show you
I'll know you the best I can know you, baby, as long as I know you

What kind of love never turns away
What kind of love never makes you pay, hears you when you pray

What kind of love makes you go out in the wind and the driving rain
What kind of love runs through your heart with a pleasure so close to pain
What kind of love, only this love that I have

This love I know is all I have (all I have)
This love I have is all I know
So I won't let go

What kind of love makes you go out in the wind and the driving rain
What kind of love runs through your heart with a pleasure so close to pain
What kind of love, only this love that I have
What kind of love, only this love that I have

RC, Will Jennings & Roy Orbison
'90

QUÉ ES AMOR? (ÉL) ES UN LOCO QUE CANTA
EN EL HURACÁN

¿QUÉ ES AMOR? (ELLA) ES UNA LOCA QUE LE
ENCANTA
CANCIÓN

Please Remember Me

When all our tears have reached the sea
A part of you will live in me
Way down inside my heart
The days keep coming without fail
A new wind is going to find your sail
That's where your journey starts

You'll find better love, strong as it ever was
Deep as the river runs, warm as the morning sun
Please remember me

Just like the waves down by the shore
We're going to keep on coming back for more
'Cause we don't ever want to stop
Out in this brave new world you seek
So many valleys and so many peaks
That I can see you up on top

You'll find better love, strong as it ever was
Deep as the river runs, warm as the morning sun
Please remember me

Remember me when you're out walking
When the snow falls high outside your door
Late at night when you're not sleeping
And moonlight falls across your floor
When I can't hurt you anymore

You'll find better love, strong as it ever was
Deep as the river runs, warm as the morning sun
Please remember me
Please remember me

RC & Will Jennings
'95

When all our tears have reached the sea
A part of you will live in me
In the ~~room~~ shelter of my heart
~~Leave~~ There'll be no bread crumbs on the trail
A new wind ~~will~~ gonna find your sail
That's how ~~That's~~ ~~and there your~~ and that's where your journey starts
The days keep coming without fail

Chorus
You'll find better love strong as it ever was
Deep as the river runs warm as the morning sun
Please remember me

Sometimes the ones we want the most
are the ones that we can't have up close
+ we don't know how to stop
Sometimes the things that we can't see
Is the very thing thats meant to be
So lets take it from top (It comes as such a shock) (from the bottom to the top)

Chorus,

Remember me when your out walkin
when snow falls high outside your door
Late at night when youre not sleepin
+ moonlight falls across your floor
when I can't hurt you any more
Please remember me
Just like the waves down by the shore
we'll keep on coming back for more
for the rest of our life
Chorus 'cause we don't ever want to stop

Time + time again ~~Beginning~~ ~~where we~~ ... we search for things that we can't see and then one day they come to be ~~That's where your~~ heart will mean

~~In~~ the brave new world you'll seek
on the valleys and the ~~peaks~~
I can see you on the top

That's where it all begins

Making Memories of Us

I'm gonna be here for you, baby, I'll be a man of my word
Speak the language in a voice that you have never heard
I want to sleep with you forever, I want to die in your arms
In a cabin by a meadow where the wild bees swarm

I'm gonna love you like nobody loves you
I'll earn your trust making memories of us

I want to honor your mother, I want learn from your pa
I want to steal your attention like a bad outlaw
I want to stand out in a crowd for you, a man among men
I want to make your world better than it's ever been

And I'm gonna love you like nobody loves you
I'll earn your trust making memories of us

We'll follow the rainbow wherever the four winds blow
There'll be a new day coming your way

I'm gonna be here for you from now on, this you know somehow
You've been stretched to the limits but it's alright now
I'm gonna make you a promise if there's life after this
I'm gonna be there to meet you with a warm, wet kiss

And I'm gonna love you like nobody loves you
And I'll earn your trust making memories of us
I'll always love you like nobody loves you
I'll win your trust making memories of us

'03

Happy New Year!
2000

SELECTED LYRICS
PART THREE

Oh, What a Beautiful World

It's the time and the place, every line on your face
It's the truth and the lie, it's to live and to die
Oh, what a beautiful world

It's a girl and a boy, and the first taste of joy
It's an old photograph of two hearts torn in half
Oh, what a beautiful world

We build our hopes up high perchance to someday fly
Across a clear blue sky to someplace new

It's a walk in the park and a shot in the dark
It's the thief in the night meets the first ray of light
Oh, what a beautiful world

We live our legends down, wake up in lost and found
Become that highway sound and roll on through

It's the rise and the fall of the clocks on the wall
It's the first and the last of your days flying past
Oh, what a beautiful world
Oh, what a beautiful world

Bluebird Wine (Revised)

Baby brought me in out off the highway
Poured my rot-gut liquor down the sink
Straightened out my crooked ways of thinking
Made it purely pleasure when I drink

And it's alright now, I just hit my stride
Right off the bat I'm drunk on Bluebird wine

Baby's up and running in the morning
Says she's got a million things to do
While I'm gone says you go get your guitar
And write some pretty song about me and you

And it's alright now, I just hit my stride
Right off the bat I'm drunk on Bluebird wine

Baby says she'd really love a party
Get some friends together feeling fine
Any friend of mine is worth his habit
A belly full of baby's Bluebird wine

And it's alright now, I just hit my stride
Right off the bat I'm drunk on Bluebird wine
And it's alright, I just hit my stride
The party just started and I'm drunk on Bluebird wine

The Damage

So, you found me at the end of my life
By the bend in the river at dawn
Have you come to my aid, are there deals to be made
Thin lines in the sand to be drawn
Now that you're here, pray tell my dear
Why it is you've come to my door
By virtue or sin should I let you in
I can't say you'll suffer no more

So, they tied you to the stake in your heart
And they taught you to treasure the pain
To keep you in place they lied to your face
And they bought you with measured disdain
Now that you've seen your part in the dream
You'll need to be lost to belong
The story that ends before it begins
Means nothing is written in stone

Once there was a time I might have been for you a guiding light
Cross my heart and hope to die a thousand needles in my eye
The damage is already done

When it's over as soon it must be
Please mention my name to the wind
The trouble I see for you and for me
Is nobody wins in the end

I was once as young and wild as you my dark-eyed woman child
How I spend my days in dread is how it is, I made my bed
I can't teach or preach or reach beyond the veil we both know well
The damage, the damage, the damage is already done

Forty Miles From Nowhere at the Bottom of The World

It rained today, clouds rolled up at dawn
All hell burst wide open, and just like that was gone
Your little lapdog chased a fox-tail squirrel
Across the main road through the wood
Some ninja on a dirt bike nearly ran him down for good

Right about now it gets quiet around here
What with nightfall in the wings
The floorboards creak and the faucets leak
But it's the emptiness that sings
The wind grows chill and then lies still
Forty miles from nowhere at the bottom of the world

November sky's a diamond-studded dome
A hundred million points of light to guide my way back home
When the moon is hanging fat and full
And all those jangly stars recede
A fold-out couch on a midnight porch is where my footsteps lead
You always said I made my bed
Forty miles from nowhere at the bottom of the world

Friend's don't call like they used to, for reasons not unkind
"Is there anything that we can do?" rings hollow down a telephone line

There's a cedar grove in back of the house halfway down the hill
A place to go to just lay low when there was precious time to fill
A few gravestones, a pre-Civil War fence and the random arrowhead
Where the beehive swarmed three summers ago
"Too wet," the old men said
So, it's me, your little lapdog and that old brindle cat
Trying to keep this place in line
And heading into town these days is the last thing on my mind

I wait for you, it's what I do
Forty miles from nowhere at the bottom of the world

56 Fury

Spit curl down his forehead
Talking 'bout how yes, it's understood
It's not just some lame six-bang grease stain
Sitting underneath the hood
Tamping down a Camel on a Zippo with a grin
Maybe wider than a country mile
Corsicana cool hand taking us to school, man
Burning up the road in style

56 Fury, built for comfort built for speed
56 Fury, along about everything you need
56 Fury

Hair stacked up and twisted
Like some beehive made in France
Seven double shots of spray net
Down for nothing left to chance
Here's what's real, cried sweet Lucille
There ain't no other boy I know
Who can even dare to hold a candle
To that loving hotrod Romeo

56 Fury, high performance built for fun
56 Fury, Lord have mercy, watch her, look at her run
56 Fury

Two-door hard-top coupe, so sleek and sexy
Make a grown man moan
Jet white streak of lightning destination long since gone
Back off V8 Ford, back off Chevrolet
Pontiac and Cadillac ain't even fit for hauling hay

56 Fury, bound for glory, seconds flat
56 Fury, somebody tell me maybe what was that
That was a 56 Fury, finest car on the road

Ain't No Two Lane
Texas Back Road
Can't Be
Long Have

on His Forehead
It's understood
Six Banger
underneath The Hood
Camel on a Zippo
wider Than a c
took us TO School
Known as Style
Built for Com
about Cory L

Simonize

Rodney Crowell

~~When the wind starts to blow + the leaves touch the ground~~

You tore through my ♡ like a tornado

Lookin for a trailer park

when vows become swords

your white trash mish mash

Short of cash culture clash

Call Michael

Hit the mark

We try to break thru the force that restrains
the ~~peace~~ love in our hearts we try to be real

We met on a Monday here it is Sunday

It happen so fast they said it wouldn't last

But what do they know it doesn't matter any how

8761

8753

Frankie Else

You stole into my heart like a thief with a cutting

Touch didn't you

Your lame brain disdain for any ~~time~~ everything

Lays the blame on you know who
~~Lays the blame~~ on me + you Frankie

Frankie Please

You tore through my heart like a tornado looking for a trailer park
Your white trash mishmash short-of-cash culture clash hit the mark
We met on a Monday, here it is Sunday
It happened so fast, they said it wouldn't last
Yeah, but what do they know, why can't they say so now?

I was racking up points in the dives and the joints on the edge of town
Shootin' pool, playing cool, trying to get some other fool to buy another round
You rattled my brain like a runaway train
You scattered my past like a dynamite blast
You're some kind of woman, Frankie, stand up and take a bow

Frankie, please don't ever give me the deep freeze
Your p's and q's and don'ts and do's
Are all the news that light my fuse
Don't change nothing, not on a dare
Ever since you hit here I've been walking on air
I'm a fool for you, Frankie, don't let me let you go

You stole into my heart like a thief with a cutting torch, did you not?
Your can't miss first kiss told me this, don't resist what you've got
All out of nowhere I'm caught in your crosshairs
Fragged, shagged, bagged, tagged
It's like I lost every battle and still I won the war

Frankie, please don't ever give me the deep freeze
In the time we've got let's tie the knot
And fire the shot that hits the spot
Lord, have mercy, hallowed be
It ain't a pretty picture but it's working on me
I'm a fool for you, Frankie, don't let me let you go

You're one-in-a-million, Frankie, that's all I need to know

Tree top 2 Lim
And
BILLY.
Low
Grass.

Treetop Slim and Billy Lowgrass

Treetop Slim was a gangling lad, stood six-foot-six at twelve
On painted pony into town, his brogan shoes scraped the ground
Talk about a rifle shot, Treetop Slim was really hot

Billy Lowgrass, he was small just barely pushing five-feet-tall
But when he drew his pistol aim, everybody know'd his name

Billy Lowgrass, better think fast,
Come on Slim, the chance is dim
They've got faster horses, grown men riding
Two young boys can't go on hiding

Treetop Slim and Billy Lowgrass, Texas Rangers dogging your ass
Hiding out in the land of pine cones, a life of crime won't last too long

Treetop Slim, it's sink or swim
Billy Low, you ought to know
They've got faster horses, grown men riding
Two young boys can't go on hiding

Treetop Slim and Billy Lowgrass, Fredonia law men are dogging your ass
Hiding out in the piney woods, robbing banks won't do you no good

Treetop Slim and Billy Lowgrass, Texas Rangers dogging your ass
Hiding out in a big pine thicket, robbing banks just ain't the ticket

Beautiful Despair

Beautiful despair is hearing Dylan when you're drunk at 3 am
Knowing that the chances are, no matter what, you'll never write like him

Oh brother

Beautiful despair is why you lean into this world without restraint
Because somewhere out before you lies the masterpiece you'd sell your soul to paint

Oh brother
What do we?
Laugh or cry?

Beautiful despair is slouching forward toward a past you might regret
All to suck the marrow out of every magic moment that you get

Beautiful despair is playing safe when you were once a rebel child
Knowing that tomorrow comes and all you've done is last another mile

Oh, brother
Oh, dear brother
Oh, my brother
What shall we?
Drink or dry?

Belfast

(for James Napier)

Jesus Talk To Mama

Jesus, talk to mama, tell her I'm alright
Tell her that I'm on the mend
Tell her I've been born again
Tell her that the future's looking bright

Do this won't you, Jesus, for I never meant to stray
Jesus, talk to mama, tell her that we'll meet again someday

Jesus, if you hear me, take a message to my ma
Tell her I'm a different man
Tell her that I'm in your hands
Tonight I beat the devil to the draw

All I'm really asking is to tell her I found you
Jesus, talk to mama, tell her that my wandering days are through

Jesus, talk to mama, tell her I'm doing good
Tell her how I kicked the blues
Tell her how it's all good news
I'm living like she always wished I would

Tell her won't you, Jesus, that the wonders never cease
Jesus, talk to mama, tell her so her soul can rest in peace

Thomas Petillo

Don't Get Me Started

We ran into trouble scamming for oil
Now the whole Middle East is coming to a boil
It's the Muslims and Kurds, Bedouin herds
Palestinians and Arabs and Jews in the news
It's too much to keep up with, it'll jangle your head
The whole situation is running way in the red

Don't get me started, I'll like as not bend you ear
Don't get me started, I just want to make one thing clear

I was born in America and I'm proud of that fact
I wish the rest of the world would get off our back
But these slick politicians, man, you've got to admit
Seem as crazy as bedbugs and don't give one whit
About a man on the street with his back to the wall
Who can't find a quarter for to make a phone call
Meanwhile, back in Washington, champagne will flow
Tell that to a homeless man with nowhere to go, I said

Don't get me started, I came into this bar to unwind
Don't get me started, I'll like as not speak my mind

The rich corporations have turned a deaf ear
They don't care who goes hungry, they've made that much clear
You see the trouble with people is we want to believe
But they can't turn a profit without tricks up their sleeve
It's the roofers and truckers, the working-class suckers
The firemen and teachers, the soldiers and preachers
Who shoulder the blows, it comes and it goes
A six-trillion-dollar debt you pay through the nose, I said

Don't get me started, I'm a drag when I've had a few drinks
Don't get me started, I don't care what anyone thinks
'Cause it makes me angry

East Timor's genocide to the core
The Indonesian legions come and give 'em what for
When the coalition army doesn't come to your aid
You might as well face it, there's no money to be made
I had a dream last night I was Secretary of Defense
And I came to the conclusion war doesn't make any sense
Yeah, but nobody heard me when I tried to rescind it
There were too many people that just didn't want to end it, I said

Don't get me started, you never know when I might stop
Don't get me started, we both need to just let this thing drop
Don't get me started
Don't get me stared, not now
Don't get me started
'Cause it makes me crazy

Glasgow Girl

I'm stuck out on the ring road, tonight the stars are crossed
If I don't find my way around soon, I'm sure to end up lost
Sheffield has that certain mix of danger and despair
I need to roll these windows down and breathe the cold night air

I said goodbye to Camden town as night was falling fast
In a borrowed and beat-up step van with a tank of petrol gas
Now I'm riding on the wrong side like some blue yank flyboy clown
Trying to read these road signs while I'm staring headlights down

Glasgow Girl, skin like milk, hair black silk, and eyes like cobalt pearl

The Glasgow girl assured me she liked my Texas drawl
And if I ever pass that way again I should be sure to call
I tracked her down to Aberdeen and I'm trying to get up north
Across the Scottish Lowlands beyond the Firth of Forth

Glasgow Girl, skin like milk, hair black silk, and eyes like cobalt pearl

The Romans built these roads to last another thousand years
And I'm riding around in circles like it starts and ends right here
The raindrops on my windshield now have turned to ice and snow
And I'm stuck out on the ring road with a million miles to go

Glasgow Girl, skin like milk, hair black silk, and eyes like cobalt pearl
Skin like milk, hair black silk, and eyes like cobalt pearl

I'm Stuck out on the Ring Road
The Petrol in my Ride
Is not Enough to Get me Back
To Scots Town on the Clyde
That Glasgow Girl Assured me
She love my Texas Drawl
But I'm stuck out on the Ring Road
Crawl

Aberdeen
I'm Stuck out on the Ring Road
& I'm Trying to Get up North
Across the Scottish Moors & Low Lands
and Beyond the Firth of Forth

my Life Became Enchanted by
The Dream that Calls me On

I'm Stuck out on the Ring Road
Tonight the Stars are Crossed
The Tinker Stole my Free will
& the Ransom note was Lost
She Holds has that Certain mix
Of Danger & Despair
I'm Stuck out on the Ring Road
& Not Getting any where (Stand a Band Hold Stare)

I'm Stuck out on the Ring Road
& Traffic's Bearing Down
I'm Driving on the Wrong Side
& Feeling Like A Clown.
Rain Drops on my Windshield
Look Like Random Gobs of Spit
I'm stuck out on the Ring Road
& Trouble Just Won't Quit

I'm sure to Crash & Burn
you'd think I'd Know myself by now
But Some Fools Never Learn

The Outsider

You don't have to be rich
I don't have to be drunk in a ditch
You don't have to be top of your class
I don't have to have huevos of brass
You don't have to be cute
I don't have to look good in a suit
You don't have to have a dog in this race
I don't have to have egg on my face

The Outsider, watching your back
The Outsider, cut me some slack
The Outsider, just a little off keel
The Outsider, something you feel

I don't have to be straight
You don't have to be something I hate
I don't have to be white as a ghost
You don't have to be dumb as a post
I don't have to be hip
You don't have to start losing your grip
I don't have to be right if your wrong
You don't have to be weak if I'm strong

The Outsider, like a coat when you're cold
The Outsider, like a friend when you're old
The Outsider, a little devil-may-care
The Outsider, just somethings that's there

You don't want to be a saint
I don't want to be something I ain't
First you get a little long in the tooth
Next you try to find the fountain of youth
It's a pain in the butt
That's the trouble when you're stuck in a rut
We don't have to find a permanent bliss
But we've got to do better than this

The Outsider, like a stone you don't throw
The Outsider, like a bomb you don't blow
The Outsider, like a mountain won't move
The Outsider, you've got nothing to prove

40 Winters

Forty winters, cold and dark, surround you like a beauty mark
A tilt of the axis says that time of year
The flush of your cheekbone says no damage here
The first time I saw you there was ice on the ground
A girl in a greenhouse said paradise found
For forty winters

Forty winters straight in line, were you not my valentine?
Orange blossoms, sandalwood, oak-moss and musk
To fragrant your senses from daylight till dusk
You made the simple life fit for a king
And oatmeal by candle light, a beautiful thing
For forty winters

Why can't I break the spell, shake you and make you well?
What is it blinding me that keeps you from finding me?
I know you're in there, you haven't gone somewhere
That God only knows about leaving me frozen out
Darling, I promise you this, I won't let you drown in the mist

Forty winters, cold and drear, could not age you one short year
It's like you're trapped 'neath a bell jar as big as the earth
And I'm running to reach you for all that I'm worth
I'll bathe you and feed you and I'll tend to your grace
But don't make me leave you in such a dark place

I'm drunk on the bitterness that sorrow demands
And I know that tomorrow is out of my hands
Until we're together I'll sleep in the snow
And I'll love you forever for that's all I know about
Forty winters, forty winters, forty winters
Forty winters, forty winters, forty winters
. . . .

(for Laneal)

Epictetus Speaks (Dancing Circles Round the Sun)

Disregard what don't concern you
Don't let disappointment turn you
Avoid adopting other people's view
Know what you can and can't control
Don't let envy take a toll
It's nothing more than weather passing through

When your back's against the wall
When you're headed for a fall
The table's set to make a run
Dancing circles 'round the sun

Through action wisdom is revealed
Too much talk is like a shield
In silence lies the keys to how we grow
When focused on the truth at hand
The critics try to make you bland
But they don't understand what they don't know

Make your own cracks in the sky
Grit your teeth and learn to fly
When the right thing has been done
You'll dance circles 'round the sun

Forgive the ones who meant to harm you
Don't let superstition charm you
Conform your wishes only to what's real
Your reputation doesn't matter
Let idle gossip chirp and chatter
No one else can tell you how to feel

In between the masks you wear
Wash your face and comb your hair
You're not hurting anyone
Dancing circles 'round the sun

Your mind cries out to God alone
Please send me someone I can own
Your soul says, son, you're walking on thin ice
Possession in the broadest sense
Compounded by coincidence
All it takes is one roll of the dice

In between the good and bad
Think of all the fun you had
You're not hurting anyone
Dancing circles 'round the sun

Evolution comes in fits
It stops and starts, it coughs and spits
Picasso and Miles Davis come to mind
Two artists, bold unbridled passion
No concern for fad or fashion
Sexy beasts in love with womankind

Bend the rule until it breaks
Stand your ground until it shakes
That's the way to get things done
Dancing circles 'round the sun

Hey sod convention, let's have fun
Dancing circles 'round the sun

your mind cries out to God alone
Please send me someone I can own
your soul says son your walkin on thin ice
Possession in the Broadest Sense
Is Governed / Founded / Compounded By Coincidence
All it takes is one Roll of the Dice

In Between the Good + Bad
Lies a lot of things you had
It's the same for everyone
Dancing circles Round the sun

Bend a Rule until it Breaks
Stand your Ground until it shakes
That's the way to get things done

De construction is your Friend
Revision till the End
That's the way

Evolution comes in fits
It stops and starts Cough's and spits
Picasso + Miles Davis come to mind
to deconstruct the art of living
you make the most of what your

Behold the art of Recon struction

Behold the Artists Bridled Passion
with no concern for Fad or Fashion
Sexy Beast's I Love with
Woman Kind

The Artists Bold and Bridled Passion
No Concern For Fad or Fashion

your Eyes Behold the Sexy Beast
+ all your Passions are Released

When North is South + West is East
you must observe the Sexy Beast
who's art of deconstruction draws the Line

Make your own Sketches of Spain
Still Life twisting in the Rain
Theres so much left to Be Done

Fuck Convention
Let's Have Some Fun
Dancing Circles
Round + Res

Dis Regard what Dont Concern you
Don't Let Dissapointment turn you
Avoid Adopting Other Peoples View
Know what you Can and Can't Control
Dont Let envy take a toll
It's Nothing more than weather Passing thru

When your Backs Against the wall
When your Headed For a Fall
The Tables set to make a Run
Dancing Circles Round the Sun

Through Action wisdom Is Revealed
Too much talk is like a Shield
In Silence Lies the Keys to How we Grow
When Focused on the Truth at Hand
The Critics try to make you Bland
But They Dont understand what they dont know
~~Big old~~ Cracks in the Sky
& your Learning How to Fly
When the Right thing Has Been Done
You Dance Circles Round the Sun

Forgive the ones who meant to Harm you
Dont Let ~~Dissapointment~~ Superstition Charm you
Conform your wishes only to what's Real
Your Reputation Doesn't matter
Let Idle Gossip Chirp and Chatter
No one Else Can tell you How you Feel
In Between the masks we wear
There's a tendency to stare
You're not Hurting Anyone
Dancing Circles Round the Sun

Brownwood Coliseum
RODNEY CROWELL
SHOW & DANCE
SEPT 3
9 PM
RepublicBank Brownwood

Hank DeVito

Hank DeVito

DAD
TO THE
BONE

COLLABORATIONS

EMMYLOU HARRIS

painting by Ray Martin

He came along when I needed to sing my heart out so we did.

He came along when I was looking for words to feed my soul, and his did.

He came to be a poet, not of a homeland but a bunch of pilgrims

On their way to finding one, which they did.

So, sometimes when I wonder if anything really makes a difference, which it does,

I just smile and remember how we rocked those joints up and down the coast of California.

— Emmylou Harris

Oh Amarillo

My baby never was the cheating kind
But it wasn't 'cause the ladies didn't try
Everywhere we go, they're walking 'round him slow
Giving him a flutter and a sigh
I got him past that redhead in Atlanta
I walked all over that black-eyed Cajun queen
Outside of Amarillo he found his thrill, I'll tell ya
I lost him to a jukebox and a pinball machine

> Oh, Amarillo, what you want my baby for?
> Oh, Amarillo, now he won't come home no more
> You done played a trick on me
> Hooked him in the first degree
> He'll put in another quarter, punch Dolly and Porter
> While he racks up fifty thousand on the pinball machine

Only that we hadn't stopped for coffee
If someone hadn't played "The Window Up Above"
He would still be mine today but he heard those fiddles play
One look and I knew it must be love
That old pinball machine was over in the corner
He saw the lights and just had to hear them ring
He never was the same after he won his first free game
I lost him to a jukebox and a pinball machine

> Oh, Amarillo, what you want my baby for?
> Oh, Amarillo, now he won't come home no more
> You done played a trick on me
> Hooked him in the first degree
> He'll put in another quarter, punch Dolly and Porter
> While he racks up fifty thousand on the pinball machine

Emmylou & RC
'75

Tulsa Queen

I heard a train in the Tulsa night
Calling out my name, looking for a fight
She's come a long, long way, got a longer way to go
Tell me how a train from Tulsa has got a right to know

She sings a song so sad and high
And the Tulsa Queen don't ever lie
She don't care where she goes, don't care where she's been
And the Tulsa Queen ain't crying 'cause I won't see you again

I want to ride like the Tulsa Queen
Calling out to you like she calls to me
As far away from Tulsa as these ten wheels can be

Lately I speak your name too loud
Each time it comes up in a crowd
I know it when I do, the Tulsa Queen and you
Are gone

And I want to ride like the Tulsa Queen
Calling out to you like she calls to me
As far away from Tulsa as these ten wheels can be

Emmylou & RC

Waltz Across Texas Tonight

The wind can blow cold, it moans and it cries
And it carries the sound of a thousand goodbyes
But if you listen tonight on that high lonesome plain
You'll just hear my voice as it calls out your name

You've been on a road that just don't seem to end
Where that broken old heart of yours won't ever mend
You crossed over bridges and watched them all burn
So many rivers and so much to learn

The moon is so full, the stars are so bright
My hand is steady, my touch is light
Look in my eyes and hold on real tight
I'll waltz you my darling across Texas tonight

We've both had some hard luck and loves that's gone wrong
When the ghosts in the shadows and the night takes too long
Oh but there's still gold in them hills, and life on this earth
Shake hands and come out dancing for all that you're worth

The moon is so full, the stars are so bright
My hand is steady, my touch is light
Look in my eyes and hold on real tight
And I'll waltz you my darling across Texas tonight
Yes, I'll waltz you my darling 'cross Texas tonight

Emmylou & RC

Waltz Across Texas
The wind can blow cold
when it carries the sound of
but if you listen tonight on that
you'll just hear my voice

you've been on a road that
where that broken ol' heart of
oh but you'll never know what's
with your face to the
feet standing still

The moon is so full
The stars are so bright
And my hand is gentle
my touch is light
Look in my eyes, hold
and I'll waltz you my
across Texas tonight

we both have known hard
when the ghosts take the
oh but there's still gold in
and life in this earth
so shake hands & come out
for all that you're

The Traveling Kind

We don't all die young to save our spark
From the ravages of time
But the first and last to leave their mark
Someday become the traveling kind

In the wind are names of poets passed
Some were friends of yours and mine
And to those unsung we lift our glass
May their songs become the traveling kind

We were born to brave this tilted world
With our hearts laid on the line
Be it Waycross boy or red dirt girl
The songs become the traveling kind

There are mountains worth their weight in gold
Mere mortals dare not climb
Come ye gypsy, sainted, sinners, bold
And claim them for the traveling kind

When the music slowly starts to fade
Into the light's last soft decline
Let us lie down in that evening shade
And rest among the traveling kind
The song goes on for the traveling kind

RC, Emmylou & Cory Chisel

You Can't Say We Didn't Try

Just because we're scared doesn't mean we're wrong
The world won't end today if both of us move on
But didn't we have a time, you can't take that away
We've had a change of mind, I think it's safe to say

That I've been holding on to you and you've been holding on to me
'Cause neither of us wants to be the first to say goodbye
So it goes, we must admit, how we both thought that this was it
Though we couldn't make the pieces fit, you can't say we didn't try

Close the window, pull the shade, turn the key and lock the door
We'd best forget the plans we made, we don't live here anymore
Maybe somewhere down the line we'll remember who we were
Another place, another time when some old feeling starts to stir

I've been holding on to you and you've been holding on to me
'Cause neither of us wants to be the first to say goodbye
And so it goes we've grown apart, guess you could say we lost the heart
And even though we came up short, you can't say we didn't try

RC, Emmylou & Cory Chisel

The Weight of the World

Smokin' down the track come a Fireball Mail
Blowin' coal so black can't even see the rail
Forty tons of steel behind a drivin' wheel
Pulls the weight of the world

Comin' up the road, another rubber tire Ford
Got us hooked on oil 'til the pipeline blowed
Such a shame to see, adding World War Three
To the weight of the world

Knock the top off a mountain without nary a shrug
Poison us up a river with the devil's own sludge
It's the American dream but if you live down stream
Here comes the weight of the world

Ton of plastic bottles headed out to sea
Bound to build an island, thanks to you and me
Another man-made pearl full of junk we hurl
Atop the weight of the world

Got to feed the baby, recompense the rent
Before we figure out where all the money went
Where there's a piper to pay, can't get away
From the weight of the world

Look up in the sky, is it a bird or plane?
Technological eye drove us all insane
Since they sent us reelin' the only thing we're feeling
Is the weight of the world
First we get so numb then we all succumb
To the weight of the world

RC & Emmylou

Higher Mountains

You're out there among the stars, it never will seem right
If I could get to where you are I'd be there tonight
Were you just a dream I had? How am I to know?
I can't hold you in my arms and I can't let you go

Higher Mountains, deeper valleys, longer rivers stand between us now
I could climb that jagged peak, I could cross that great divide
If I knew that you'd be waiting for me on the other side

The days pass by my window now, oh but nights like these are rough
I can feel you in my heart but that's not close enough
If I could hear you breathe again, the comfort of your sigh
I'd gladly trade tomorrow in on one more last goodbye

Higher mountains, deeper valleys, longer rivers stand between us now
When I rise above this earth and the firmaments collide
When I pass through heaven's gateway let me enter as your bride
Bluebonnets in my hair that you gathered for me there

RC, Emmylou & Will Jennings

If You Lived Here You'd be Home Now

I don't wonder where you are, I don't even care
Things have changed, they're not the same, you're not my cross to bear
I see you in a different light, the truth got through somehow
If you lived here you'd be home now

If you lived here you'd be on the phone talking to your momma
Saying you ain't gone and left here yet, but someday you was gonna
The day I pledged my love to you sure raised a few eyebrows
If you lived here you'd be home now

You keep wanting me to be something that I'm not
What you see is what you get and I'm the one you got
I'm tired of breaking these rocks up in this field my heart won't plow
If you lived here you'd be home now

If you lived here you'd be at my throat like every time before
Slinging them old hurtful words and walking on out the door
Sometimes I think I want you back but there ain't no way, no how
If you lived here you'd be home now
It's time I did the right thing and released you from your vow
If you lived here you'd be home now
If you lived here you'd be home now

Emmylou & RC

(thanks to Steuart Smith)

La Danse de la Joie

Oh mama, Oh papa, la danse de la joie
Papa, mama
The night is young the stars are strung
La danse de la joie mama papa

Paint me on that lipstick smile, dance around the house in style
Wiggle, wag them pretty legs, come on, gal, don't make me beg

Go on and get your lampshade on, rattle that old bag of bones
Cut you a rug all which-a-way, mon cher ami bon temps rouler'
Bon temps rouler' mon cher ami c'est moi et toi toujours en vie
Is anything in life more sweet than you and me and four left feet?

Oh mama, Oh papa, la danse de la joie
Papa, mama
The night is young, the stars are strung
La danse de la joie, mama, papa

Every now and then the blues run off with my dancing shoes
The only one thing that brings 'em back is right there in your flour sack

Hand me down my rolling pin, give me that ole poor boy grin
I'll pat out some biscuit dough, vous et moi les fais do do
Vous et moi les fais do do je vais mettre sur Fats Domino
La danse del le joie c'est toujours, plus ain't no one home but me and you

Oh mama, oh papa, la danse de la joie
Papa, mama
The night is young, the stars are strung
La danse de la joie, mama, papa

Emmylou & RC

FOR ROONEY
12.15.87

WRITING SONGS IS MYSTERIOUS STUFF -
SOMETIMES YOU WRITE FOR NO REASON
SOMETIMES YOU WRITE TILL IT HURTS
SOMETIMES YOU WRITE WITH A VENGEANCE
BUT ITS ALL JUST A SEARCH FOR THE TRUTH
SOMETIMES ALL IT TAKES IS A SHOT IN THE DARK
TO SEE THE LIGHT.

GUY

Once More With Caution

I can't stop the rain from falling but you can come inside
Until the clouds have broken and there's sunshine in your eyes
Those old fair-weather friends will treat you cold as ice
I can't stop the rain from falling but I can dry your eyes

Once more with caution thrown to the wind
Long time no see, so far so good, so come on in

Man, you sure look lonesome, I guess you been to town
Where you wore out every barstool on your merry-go-round
I won't ever say I told you so, Lord, help the fool who tries
I can't stop the rain from falling but I can dry your eyes

Once more with caution thrown to the wind
Long time no see, so far so good, so come on in

RC-Guy Clark & Susanna Clark
Started in 1976 and finished in 2020

GUY CLARK

Murder of Crows Murder of Crows
were a Murder of Crows

Baby Rattlesnake
Taste Sweet
Skin and Bones 2x & not much meat
Better watch out
Little Baby Rattlesnake Better watch out

H & J Built a barren wind nest
In a windmill derrick way out west
Made it from scraps from a lone fence line
It was a work of art only one of its kind
H & J were some birds of a feather
Braving the weather

Nothin between you & the North Pole
But barbed wire fence

H & J were some tough ol' birds

Birds
A sky
This was out around
Lubbock as the crow
Flies
Sinnin caw caw blues
Cross a cold gray skies
when the dust bowl
settled

Scrapin up scraps
Down a lone fence
Line

But around Lubbock
when the dust bowl settle
Two tough old birds
Built a house of metal
Made some heavy metal

Heckle & Jeckle were a murder of crows
A murder of crows yes a murder of crows
Heckle & Jeckle were a murder of crows
with a
A murder of crows
When things
You know anything goes

Caw Caw Blues

Heckle and Jeckle built a barbed wire nest
In a windmill derrick way out west
Scoopin' up scraps down a long fence line
It was a work of art, only one of its kind
Way out around Lubbock as the john crow flies
Ole Heckle and Jeckle built a sky-high rise
Heckle and Jeckle, so cold jet black
You could see 'em at night in the cactus, Jack

Murder of crows, murder of crows, two old birds make a murder of crows
Everyone knows anything goes, ole Heckle and Jeckle make a murder of crows

Catchin' baby rattlesnakes two-by-two
Make a little pot of that rattlesnake stew
Little baby rattlesnakes better watch out
Ole Heckle and Jeckle are out and about

Murder of crows, murder of crows, two old birds make a murder of crows
Everyone knows anything goes, ole Heckle and Jeckle make a murder of crows

Scarecrow standing in a tall corn patch
Heckle and Jeckle got nary a scratch
Eatin' like kings nearly all day long
Dodging that buckshot, singing that song
Caw caw blues, caw caw blues
Ten'll get you twenty if you're countin' by twos
Barbed wire palace full of magpie chicks
Ole heckle & Jeckle steady getting their kicks

Murder of crows, murder of crows, two old birds make a murder of crows
Everyone knows anything goes, ole Heckle and Jeckle make a murder of crows

Daddy's in the kitchen in his everyday shoes
Sittin' down singing them caw caw Blues

RC & Guy Clark
'16

501
224
9655

Coming Home

12803
L Rock St Charles Blvd
72211

We Go on Living Any Way that we Can

Ive Got An ol Blue Shirt It Suits me Just Fine
I Like the Way it Feels So I Wear it all the Time
I Got An ol Guitar Wont Ever Stay in Tune
I Like the Way it Sounds in A Dark and Empty Room
Ive Got A Rain on my window Sings So Sweet
Got the Sky Above me and the Ground Below my Feet
I Dont Need to Know the Way things might Have Been
Ive Seen Enough to Know this ~~Story Wont End~~ This story never ends

I Like Things that Work
I Like Things that Hold up
I Like the Things you Know Wont Ever Let you Down
I Like things that Feel
Things you Know Are Real
I Like the things that Make the world Keep turnin Round

Ive Got A Beat up Truck that Runs Just Like A Top
I Got the Feeling it Aint Ever Gonna Stop
I Dont Like Shoes you Cant Wear in the Dirt
If its Love thats True Sometimes its Gonna Hurt
Ive Got A woman I Love Shes Crazy and Paints Like God
Shes Got a Playground Sense of Justice She Dont Give odds
She Cuts Right Through to the Truth Like A Pocket Knife
Reminds me of my youth Shes my wife

Ive Got A Deck of Cards all Dog eared + marked
Got A tatoo of the one the Broke my Heart
Got Some Memories I Dont Ever want to Lose
And A Few Good Friends that time ~~[illegible]~~ could not Confuse

Got Some Memories I Never Could Replace
And A Few Good Friends To Help me find my Place

Ive Got A Beat up Truck
cranky ol son of A Bitch
I Guess I went too Far when I Run it in the Ditch
I Got A tatoo with Her name Right thru th ♡ my Soul
I Think Everything She touches turns to Gold

I Aint Stupid I Just Dont Know no Better

Ive Got A Feeling I Dont Ever want to Lose

I Got A Real Good Friend whos Seen me At my worst
He Cant tell if im A Blessing or A curse
He Always turns up when the Others are Down
+ Thats the Kind of Friend I want to Have Around

Stuff That Works

I've got an old blue shirt that suits me just fine
I like the way it feels so I wear it all the time
I've got an old guitar won't ever stay in tune
But I like the way it sounds in a dark and empty room

I've got an old pair of boots that fit my feet just right
I can work all day and dance all night
I've got a new used car that runs just like a top
I get the feeling it ain't ever gonna stop

Stuff that works, stuff that holds up
The kind of stuff you don't hang on the wall
Stuff that's real, that stuff you feel
The stuff you always reach for when you fall

I've got a pretty good friend who's seen me at my worst
He can't tell if I'm a blessing or a curse
But he always shows up when the chips are down
That's the kind of stuff I like to be around

Stuff that works, stuff that holds up
The kind of stuff you don't hang on the wall
Stuff that's real, that stuff you feel
The stuff you always reach for when you fall

There's a woman I love, she's crazy and paints like God
She has a playground sense of justice, she don't give odds
I've got a tattoo with her name right through my soul
I think everything she touches turns to gold

Stuff that works, stuff that holds up
The kind of stuff you don't hang on the wall
Stuff that's real, that stuff you feel
The stuff you always reach for when you fall

RC & Guy Clark
'92

(Eamon) Home & Dry

Eamon swallowed anchor and stepped himself ashore
Set seaboot down on cobblestone he'd never trod before
A low fog on the harbor did obscure the rigging lights
And the terra firma tavern cast a soft glow on the night

Sing fare-thee-well, calm seas or swell
Red evening sky, home and dry

Eamon went to sea for life the day he turned fourteen
On a merchant cargo steamer bound for Kwajalein
By way of Cartagena he wound up in Istanbul
Nineteen times around the horn would make a Dutchman drool

Old seaman's tale, stove by a whale
Set sail and fly, home and dry

He left a girl in Halifax who waited all her life
Wearing out the widow's walk ne'er to be his wife
Why Eamon chose the sailor's life only sailors know
Once the sea gets in your blood it will not let you go

Eamon headed inland where he couldn't smell the sea
Where they'd never seen a boat is where he meant to be
They dressed him in his pea coat and pulled his sea boots on
Stitched him in his hammock and sent him sailing home

Sing fare-thee-well, calm seas or swell
Red evening sky, home and dry
Sing high, sing low, sing soft, sing slow
Weigh anchor aye, he's home and dry

RC & Guy Clark
'05

I'll Show Me

It's lady's night at the Blue Gazelle
Local talent looks alive and well
All dressed up with my slack britches on
Don't get lucky, man, there's something wrong
Caddo pool hall down the Rue De Nowhere
Eight shots loaded, yeah, man I've been there
"Hey, watch this" is what I said to the pool shark
I can make it shooting in the dark

> A hundred dollars on an eight-ball call shot
> Can't scratch now 'cause that's all I've got
> I'll show me, I'll show me

Man, seeking unemployment
No gig too big to blow
Self-destruct for own enjoyment
Another knuckleheaded way to go
Blame a woman for the way I am
Much too easy, no thank you, man
How'd I ever get this far, you might ask
I'm here to tell you it was no small task

> I don't need a map to show me where
> I should be 'cause I don't care
> I'll show me, I'll show me

I kind of see myself as a young Richard Burton
Reading Dylan Thomas to some Welsh coquette
Drinking whiskey in a Swansea tavern
Me and trouble make a sure-fire bet
Well, how about this then, I'm a suave bullfighter
Or maybe a war correspondent for the BBC
Why, aye, man my load feels lighter
Another Jameson'd set me free

I don't want to have to feel or think
Bartender, pour me one more drink
I'll show me, I'll show me
Ain't it always like the old man said
Keep it simple or you'll wind up dead
I'll show me, I'll show me, I'll show me, I'll show me

RC & Guy Clark
'14

The Partner Nobody Chose

She's a melody in search of the words "I love you"
She's a rose with no room to grow
She's a light in the night with nowhere to shine
She's the partner that nobody chose

She's tried and she's tried
And she's tried to keep on trying
And everything she's tried fell apart
She's loved and she's loved
And she'd love to keep on loving
But every man she loved broke her heart

She's a melody in search of the words "I love you"
She's a rose with no room to grow
She's a light in the night with nowhere to shine
She's the partner that nobody chose

She's fallen and stumbled, stumbled and fallen
No one picked her up when she fell
She's stood up with hopes up
That someone would show up
Someday you never can tell

She's a melody in search of the words "I love you"
She's a rose with no room to grow
She's a light in the night with nowhere to shine
She's the partner that nobody chose

She a refuge where nobody goes
She's lonesome and nobody knows

RC & Guy Clark
'80

Our Little Town

If you're just passing through there's not much to do in our little town
If you're moving too fast you're not gonna last in our little town
The man on the street has a light in his eye and a shine on his shoes
There's not much of a dark side here, I just want to make that clear

Hey, our little town is a real fine place
Hey, our little town has a style and a grace
In our little town we're not gathering dust
Hey, our little town is a face you can trust
Take a good look at us in our little town

So, you've made some mistakes you can put on the brakes in our little town
If you've been living in vain why not get off the train in our little town
The ways of the world are like dust on a windshield, you just wipe 'em away
And see how it feels to be right where you wanta be

Hey, our little town is a real fine place
Hey, our little town has a style and a grace
In our little town we're not gathering dust
Hey, our little town is a face you can trust
Take a good look at us in our little town

In our little town we've got nothing to hide, you see
And if I were you there'd be no place I'd rather be

Hey, our little town is a place in the sun
In our little town we don't hurt anyone
In our little town we will tell you no lies
Hey, our little town looks you right in the eye
We never say die in our little town

RC & Guy Clark
'95

ROSANNE CASH

I admired Rodney as a songwriter long before I knew him. In truth, I felt far more than just "admiration," which implies observation with a kind of detached pleasure. I was not detached. I got as close as I could to every couplet, every melody, every drop of Bluebird wine, every slippery slope on which he tried to gain control again, and every traveling man who bolted out of Louisiana on a loping rhythm. I also felt something very different from pleasure when I absorbed his songs. I was tormented with longing to understand how he did what he did, how he could express deep feeling without ever crossing the line into squeamish sentimentality, how he could evoke a character or a scene in just a few strokes of the pen, and how he could choose every word so precisely that consonants became drumbeats, and vowels became keens and cries, or winks and nods.

Years later, when we were married, the first song we wrote together was one I had started, and he helped finish, called "Looking for a Corner." I began it in a sort of navel-gazing, tortured-English-student mood, a style in which I was far too comfortable, but he saw the potential and helped elevate it to an ethereal but universal rumination. That was a lesson in using my feelings without letting them disarm me of my skills as a writer and musician. Here was poetry and melody that was more rigorous, and more emotionally muscular and disciplined.

The last song Rodney and I wrote together, "When the Master Calls the Roll," was a co-write with John Leventhal, to whom I've been married for more than a quarter century. John wrote the aching melody, rooted in an old folk tradition, and Rodney and I wrote the lyrics. Any personal awkwardness between the three of us has long since dissipated, and the experience of working together was a full-circle exploration layered in unexpected and satisfying ways, both personally and musically. It became one of my favorite songs in my entire forty-plus years of songwriting.

The first verse was taken nearly verbatim from an ad in the personals section of a nineteenth century newspaper Rodney had come across. Rodney and I sat at my kitchen table and worked out the narrative from there—a story about William and Mary Anne, my real Civil War ancestors, framed as an Appalachian ballad. We put rhyme to the struggle for union—of a couple and a country. We adapted the language slightly to better convey the era and the tradition. We even used the word "whence," which initially made John wince.

The song and the characters obsessed me during the few days of writing. I couldn't see how the story ended and what would happen to William and Mary Anne. I was standing in the shower one day and the last verse came to me whole—a rare gift. I realized that our soldier William was writing his own eulogy. It was deeply moving. The next time Rodney and I met in my kitchen, I told him I had the last verse, and I sang it to him. He recoiled when he heard me rhyme the words "came" and "again."

"You really want to end the song with a soft rhyme?"

He cringed. "It's such a good song. We should end with a solid, hard rhyme."

I understood his objection. I respected rhyme schemes and their increments as much as he, and I knew the satisfaction of hearing a solidly rhymed couplet that didn't slightly bend the vowels land on the ear with authority. I wavered for a moment, but in my mind, it was the only thing William could say. William didn't give a damn about soft rhymes. I dug in my heels.

Rodney relented, graciously. Maybe he recognized that the creative ruthlessness which he himself modeled to me decades ago was fully assimilated on my part, and he decided to be a gentleman about it. I imagine he knows that a good deal of my sense of honor for the truth of a song, and rigor in the process, began when I was drunk on Bluebird wine, looking to gain control, and following every traveling man who left Louisiana in the broad daylight.

— Rosanne Cash

When the Master Calls the Roll

Girl with hair of flaming red seeking perfect lover
For to lie down on her feather bed no secrets to uncover
Must be gentle, must be strong with disposition sunny
As faithful as the day is long and careful with his money
And so the open letter read the newsboy did deliver
Three months later plans were made to wed down by the James River

Lo, the season may come, lo the season may go
What love has joined together will forever be made whole
When the master calls the roll

Oh, my darling William Lee take me to the altar
I don't have strength to watch you as you leave but my love will never falter
Oh, my darlin' Mary Ann, the march to war is calling
Somewhere across these southern lands are bands of brothers falling
My tender bride, the tides demand that I leave you with your mother
My father's musket in one hand and your locket in the other

Lo, the season may come, lo the season may go
Beware the storm clouds gather, take heed dear mortal soul
When the master calls the roll

But can this union be preserved, the soldier boy was crying
I will never travel back to her but not for lack of trying
It's the love of one truehearted lass that made the boy a hero
But a rifle ball and cannon blast that cut him down to zero
Oh, Virginia, whence I came, I'll see you when I'm younger
And I'll know you by your hills again, this time from six feet under

Lo, the season may come, lo the season may go
What man has torn asunder will someday be made whole
When the master calls the roll
Though the storm clouds gather let the union be made whole
When the master calls the roll

Rosanne Cash, John Leventhal & RC
'14

I Hardly Know How to be Myself

Go out and hear a band at some club downtown
Walk home in the rain and let it soak me down
Smile and shuffle past all the faces at the door
I hardly know how to be myself anymore

I wonder where you are, do I exist for you?
Or if that pain that never quits ever gets you too
I think about my life and what it's headed for
I hardly know how to be myself anymore

> I know how to chase the night away
> Show no feelings by the light of day
> I know how to keep it all intact
> Tears may fall but there's no holding back

Time runs by me like a river cold
Sends a shiver way down in my soul
I see my past just like a mask I wore
I hardly know how to be myself anymore

> I know how to face the night alone
> Keep my distance on the telephone
> I know how to get my crying done
> Tears may fall but I don't show no one

I go out and hear a band at some club on down the street
Shake the hand of all the people that I meet
I hope they find what they're all looking for
I hardly know how to be myself anymore

RC & Rosanne Cash
'90

Hank DeVito

Looking For a Corner (to Back my Heart Into)

Trouble when you're searching and you ain't so very young
You don't fit in to table talk and you can't hold back your tongue
You have what they all desire, so you must want it too
I'm looking for a corner to back my heart into

Trouble when they know you by your face or just your name
They count the times you stumble when you barely know the game
You know you never asked for this, someone who looks like you
I'm looking for a corner to back my heart into

I just want to find, while there's still time
Some peace of mind that I can hold onto
I'm not looking for some magic door
There waiting for someone to push me through

Trouble when the ones you love don't know how to love you back
You're forever climbing icy walls and forever falling back
You're not even lying and they don't believe it's true
I'm looking for a corner to back my heart into

Trouble when your heartaches don't hurt you anymore
And there's nothing like the passion that you felt so strong before
You have what they all desire but you don't want it too
I'm looking for a corner to back my heart into

Rosanne Cash & RC
'80

Real Woman

I don't want to be a star, I don't want to talk through glass
I don't want to check my appearance in your eyes
I don't need a million bucks, baby, it don't take much
I don't want to play the princess all the time

I want to be a real woman, changing every day
I want to be a real woman, real in every way
I want to be a real woman

I don't want to be admired, I don't want to fake my smile
I don't want to use my charm to disarm you
You don't have to spin your wheels, I know how that feels
You don't have to pass some test to impress me

I want to be a real woman, changing every day
I want to be a real woman, real in every way
I want to be a real woman

Real is how I deal with what I deal with
Real is how I feel when I know how I'm feeling

I don't want to be a man, I just want to be what I am
I don't want to hide my light so yours keeps shining
If you don't want to face the truth you're not gonna like what I do
You're not gonna make or break me, so don't start trying

I want to be a real woman, changing every day
I want to be a real woman, real in every way
I want to be a real woman

Rosanne Cash & RC
'90

Looking For You

Walked the streets until my heart hit the ground
There's no relief whenever you're not around
I hit the taverns where we both used to go
But it don't help me when the night's moving slow
And I'm looking for you, looking for you

I search the city for the girl I once knew
It's such a pity that there's no one like you
I tried to see my way to forget your name
I've turned to strangers but it's still not the same

I'm just looking for you (in the heart of this town)
Looking for you (and you're nowhere around)
Looking for you (in the still of the night)
Looking for you (but you're nowhere in sight)

I can see you in the shadows, I can hear you when the wind blows
And if it's all I ever do I'll keep looking for you

Exchanging glances from a sidewalk café
So many chances but you don't look my way
I search the windows for the face I can't find
Can't seem to drive your memory out of my mind

Because I'm looking for you (in the heart of this town)
Looking for you (and you're nowhere around)
Looking for you (in the still of the night)
Looking for you (but you're nowhere in sight)
I'm looking for you (in the village below)
Looking for you (where did you go)
Looking for you (on the east and west side)
Where do you hide?

RC & Rosanne Cash
'85

WILL JENNINGS

Who Could Say No

We took the wild nights for better or worse
Hell-bent and love struck, a blessing and curse
Those were the last days of oh, yes, we can
You and the world in the palm of my hand

Then time flips a coin on the passion you craved
Heads you'll be damned, tails you'll be saved
Same goes for the freedom to freefall from grace
And only to end up in such a dark place

I don't blame you
Walking away was the right thing to do
I don't blame me
You with your hunger, me with my thirst
You're fearless and fragile, my dare to go first
It's damn the torpedoes, get on with the show
The first one to get there, the last one to go
Who could say no?
Who could say no?

Whispering shadows lie still in the grass
The moon on a platter, the stars under glass
In love welded places that never will part
The life and the heat of you still in my heart

I don't blame you
I'd rather die young for the good that would do
I don't blame me
You took what you wanted, no more and no less
Part angel of mercy, part beautiful mess
With now and forever to soften the blow
I'll always be with you wherever you go
Who could say no?
We took the highlife, for better or worse
Love thirsty chapter and unwritten verse

RC & Will Jennings
'14-'20

When the Blue Hour Comes

The good times are all gone
The night keeps coming on so strong
You can't hold on, no matter what you do
Will there be someone who cares for you
When the blue hour comes

When your restless heart
Tears your world apart
And everywhere you turn it's falling down on you
Will there be a light that shines for you
When the blue hour comes

When the blue hour comes for you
If there's anything that you would have me do
Just call on me and I'll be coming through
I will always be there for you
When the blue hour comes

Good times can't last forever, sometimes it's now or never
Darling, reach out for me, you know where I'll be
I will always be there for you
When the blue hour comes

When the blue hour comes for you
If there's anything that you would have me do
Just call on me and I'll be coming though
I will always be there for you
When the blue hour comes
When the blue hour comes

RC, Will Jennings & Roy Orbison

Fever on the Bayou

Jole' Blon', Louisiana queen
Brought up on the bayou, bustin' at the seams
She moves me, says I move her too
Once we get it started there's nothing we won't do

Baby, when she roll me, fever on the bayou
When she gets ahold me, mucho-me-o-my-oh
Louisiana moon glow, way up in the sky-oh
I love to see her coming, hate to see her go

Creole belle, dancing in the rain
I love to hear her laughing, I love to hear her sing
I've got money, I've got lots of time
She makes me feel so funny when she spends my dime

Baby, when she roll me, fever on the bayou
When she gets ahold me, mucho-me-o-my-oh
Louisiana moon glow, way up in the sky-oh
I love to see her coming, hate to see her go

She's a hurricane on the Pontchartrain
Ever since she hit here, things just ain't the same

Ali mon cher mah fe demonde
Jenaise parlay Franglais jas sui su bon vivant
Revoli au-twa avec la more
Around the kitchen table and on the cabin floor

Baby when she roll me, fever on the bayou
When she gets ahold me, mucho-me-o-my-oh
Louisiana moon glow, way up in the sky-oh
I love to see her coming, I hate to see her go

RC & Will Jennings
'84–'14 (thirty years in the making)

264
0406

Baby when she Roll

Swim across
turn + toss
you da boss
on a bed of Spanish moss

Jole Blon
Grew up on the Bayou
Born Down on the Bayou

Lousiana Queen
Bustin a the seams
Best I Ever seen

she moves me
she said I move her to

once we Get It
Nothing we

Flames a little Hire
Feedin on Desire
Everthangs on Fire
Burnin up

Lousiana moon

my money's on

Love to Hear Her talk

man she make me Slip
make me Slide
make me feel
like I'm Burnin inside

Mornin Comes Lousiana Sun

Bass are Jumpin

The world

She wakes up

Daylight Comes Lousiana Morass
Bird/Bass a Jumpin Honey Bees a swarmin

deep
She wakes up River Runnin Heat
Throws Her arms around me
Pull me back to sleep

Baby when she Rolls
Every time she Rolls me Fever on the Bayou
when she Get a Hold me
Every time she Holds me Thinkin Gonna Die-O
Lousiana Moon Glow way up on the sky-O
Love to see her comin Hate to see her go

I Got money I Got Lots of Time
make me feel so funny when she spend my dime
Lips as sweet as Honey Kisses sweet as wine

Baby when she Rolls Fever on the Bayou
way down in my soul Much Ho me
Oh my O

Creole Belle
Dancin in the Rain
Love to Hear Her
Laughin Love to Hear Her Sing

The Last Waltz

Sometimes there's heartaches, and teardrops will fall
Good years and bad years, we live through it all
There's no easy answer to the trouble I see
But I'm happy just knowing you're saving the last waltz for me

Sometimes it's diamonds, sometimes it's dirt
Sometimes it's magic and sometimes it's work
There's no easy answer to the trouble I see
But I'm happy just knowing you're saving the last waltz for me

Someday we're gonna sail away, somehow we're gonna fly
Someway we'll see the light of day, shine on high

After the harvest when winter lies near
The last fiddle playing is all I can hear
There'll be no easy answer to the trouble I see
But I'm happy just knowing you're saving the last waltz for me
There's no easy answer to the trouble I see
But I'm happy just knowing you're saving the last waltz for me

RC & Will Jennings
'86

MARY KARR

I'm a Mess

Once in a while I can feel the whole world spinning
My hair twists in the wind, I can't find the brake
The clock on the dashboard is coiled like a snake
There's years flying by me at a wide-open clip
On wheels made of lightning, just barely a blip
If there's room at the top for a loser, look out
The radio's blasting a mean "Twist and Shout"
I'm a mess

At times like these a man should take a blindfold and smoke
Take a walk, take a drive, take a knee, take a dive
Take a month, take a year, take a hike, disappear
Take it on faith, whatever you get
Just close your eyes, it won't hurt a bit
The firing squad's gathered, the capitán grins
All the change in my pockets won't pay for my sins
I'm a mess

When I woke up they'd strapped me in an MRI
Black dye in my veins, head velcroed down
Foam happy slippers in a blue paper gown
The banging went on for an hour or more
Then they slid me out like a boat onto shore
The technician that caught me was sporting a smile
That said, "God grants me wisdom but the devil's got style"
I'm a mess

Now I live in New York, the Babylon of neon fire
The rats on the third rail are smokin' like char
The thunderstorm hits and I flag down a car
On the screen in Times Square I look like a wreck
As we lunge into traffic, shrinking down to a speck
The hooded skull turns saying, "Look who's alive"
And I say, "Boy, you can't scare me, just shut up and drive"
I'm a mess

Mary and RC

Rodney Crowell
mess
July 18, 2010 5:33:03 PM CDT
Mary Karr

mary, thanks for the firewood. I'm so enamored with the melody and pace of this song that I literally can't stop playing it long enough to take a shower. I've taken what you sent and hammered on it a little to make it fit the phrasing. To me, the old spoken poem in the middle works better phrasing wise (at least the first half does) and it has occurred to me that the narrator delivers the story from limbo. The cigarette and coughing might be too literal a death rattle but may yet lead us somewhere. It would be nice if the last verse comes tastefully from the afterlife.
your humble savant,
r

If the Law Don't Want You, Neither Do I

I love to see those straw dogs 'round my door
Sneakin' around my skirt tail looking for more
If you ain't running from the past
You ain't making my heart beat fast
You ain't chugging your paycheck
You ain't huggin' on my neck

I've been looking for trouble from the git
Them cowboys back where I come from won't quit
Cutting up tires on an oyster shell
Siren screaming and running like hell
Momma's on the front porch staring 'em down
Ladies at the beauty shop coming unwound

If the law don't want you, neither do I
Ain't got no time to waste my shine
On a puppet with a clip-on tie
If the law don't want you, neither do I

I hired that boy to cut my grass
Nail down a shingle but I couldn't get past
Starring at the bottom of his low-slung pants
Say he's gonna take me to the big buck dance
If the law don't want you, neither do I

I used to run wild down in Mexico
Hair jacked up and neckline plunging down low
Some snake-hip shirt-rip giving me lip
Rifling my purse, stealing my tips
There's something 'bout a man can affect that lean
Keeping his hat all yanked down mean

If the law don't want you, neither do I
Play born to lose and you light my fuse
I'm a sucker for a bald face lie
If the law don't want you, neither do I
If the law don't want you, neither do I

Mary & RC

Anything but Tame

When our feet were tough as horn and our eyes were sharp as flint
Our hearts beat like two war drums and you tracked me by my scent
'Cross a scape of shining asphalt that blacked our soles with tar
And we ran like brave Comanche on a moon-lit reservoir

And you said, I don't want to be tamed down
I just want to saddle up and ride my broomstick pony 'long some salt grass open plain
You really showed your hand popping off tin cans
With your Daisy pump air rifle and your Annie Oakley aim
You were anything but tame

You summoned me with bird calls and your scratchin' at my screen
Your mouth gone sweet with juicy fruit, tawny legs in cutoff jeans
In my straight-shift Ford Ranchero we rattled like train cars
And we slung our share of gravel 'neath a tarpaulin of stars

And you said, I don't want to be tamed down
I don't want to give an inch to fenced-off picture perfect in your billfold's window pane
No, you were born to romp in this godforsaken swamp
Dodging cottonmouths and quicksand on your tiptoes in the rain
You were anything but tame

I heard Shreveport didn't last and you lit out for LA
But when lightning claws the night up I can see you plain as day
When I want to feel you near me I crawl down off my cloud
Pole on down the bayou and cry your name out loud

And you said, I don't want to be tamed down
I don't want to tread regret or flat-out make excuses for the way I've come up lame
It should've been enough to live this off-the-cuff
On the cutting edge of nowhere where the sun goes down in flames
We were anything but tame, baby
Anything but tame

RC & Mary

Just Pleasing You

I used to get drunk all by myself
I wanted to be somebody else
There was a mask inside my mind
That I hid behind
Out on the point of no return
I crossed a bridge I could not burn
And turned down a road that led straight to
Just pleasing you

If just pleasing you is the last thing I do
I'll go to my grave nobody's slave

Most of the friends I used to know
Gave up a long, long time ago
I blew through their lives a train off track
And never looked back
I made each love a nasty joke
Every last chance a vow I broke
Then down on my knees surrendered to
Just pleasing you

If just pleasing you is the last thing I do
They'll lay me to rest knowing I've had the best

I used to get drunk all by myself
Now I set that old pain up on the shelf
And each shining day I rise up to
Just pleasing you

Just pleasing you

RC & Mary

God I'm Missing you

I heard a siren and you came to mind
You were the pretty part of us, I'm what's left behind
The equation's remainder, the last standing sign
God, I'm missing you

Your mouth still so soft, your countenance fair
Time stretches to shape you right out of thin air
But it can't hold the image, if I blink you're not there
God, I'm missing you

Are you gone forever, are you gone for good?
Or have I gone crazy just wishing you would?
Come around the next corner, step off of that train
Your old black umbrella, face half in the rain
God, I'm missing you

You're every curled rosebud enchanting my eye
Each turned-up coat collar, your gaze slides by
There's a sanded down moon in a tarpaper sky
God, I'm missing you

The night's down to nothing, the stars are withdrawn
The horizon splits open, a silvery dawn
The ghost of your breathing won't leave me alone
God, I'm missing you

Are you gone forever, are you gone for good?
Or have I gone crazy just wishing you would?
Come around the next corner, step off of the train
Your old black umbrella, face half in the rain
God, I'm missing you

God, I'm missing you

Mary & RC

Sister Oh Sister

Sister, oh, sister, I miss your shadow
I miss your shade when I was afraid
You pulled me through

Sister, big sister, you raised the standard
You set the curve, you showed the nerve
When I needed you to

Those old hairy-legged boys
Stopped making all that noise
When you beat 'em in the dirt without blinking
My fists flew in the air 'cause I knew that you'd be there
To grab 'em by the shirt without thinking

Sister, oh, sister, the whole house in shambles
You stood straight as a beam
You made a whole team out of me and you

That time we stole a car
You tried to sneak me in the bar
When I was only twelve and you were fourteen
Cross the parking lot expanse, on them oyster shells we'd dance
While some cowboy watched you twisting through the porch screen

Sister, oh, sister, you've been my seawall
You've been my flood, you're in my blood
I thank God for you

MK & RC
'09

Long Time Girl Gone By

If I could live my life again awake
Think of all the chances I could take
I'd love with all abandon just the same
'Cause that's the game

If I could cross a bridge from now till then
Open up my chest and let it in
I wouldn't fight so hard against the pain
I'd let it rain

Long time girl gone by

I couldn't take my loves the way they came
My eyes projected each one with a stain
And though they gave me more than I could spend
I wouldn't bend

Hiding in my bridal veil of smoke
I sipped my lies until I thought I'd choke
Once there was nothing left that I could steal
I had to yield

Long time girl gone by

The seconds whisper circles off the clock
Ships go sailing past and never dock
The sea rears up, collapses and withdraws
The constellations wheel and never pause
The wind winds through the small bones in my ear
I start to hear

The trees look just as pretty when they're bare
Black branches hieroglyphic in the air
The leaves they left are rotted into lace
It's all grace

Long time girl gone by

MK & RC

Hungry for Home

I love fatback and mustard greens, gobble up an onion like a peach I've seen
A pot of hot collards make a monkey out of full grown men
John cakes bigger than a catcher's mitt, butter on a biscuit, and a plate of hot grits
Soak 'em in molasses let it run on down your chin

I'm hungry for home, been gone too long
Been beat up and bent, feeling pretty much spent
Tired of making my mark everywhere I roam
I'm losing my spark, I'm hungry for home

Frito Pie and a Nehi grape sure enough leave you in tip-top shape
Ain't nothing like sitting down eatin' keep your hopes up high
Pinto bean and a black-eyed pea, boiled red cabbage and believe you me
A deviled egg and a chicken leg says you're never gonna ever say die

I'm hungry for home, been gone too long
Been beat up and bent, felling pretty much spent
Tired of making my mark everywhere I roam
But I'm losing my spark, I'm hungry for home

Popcorn shrimp, yeah, that ought'a do, next best thing to a catfish stew
Catch 'em in the river and cook 'em in the frying pan
Lemon meringue on a window sill, sweet iced tea for to drink your fill
Papa, come and get it, better live it up while we can

I'm hungry for home, been gone too long
Been beat up and bent, felling pretty much spent
Tried to make my mark everywhere I roam
But I'm losing my spark, I'm hungry for home

RC & Mary

W call

Mallory Station
Rains & Seasons
Lane Thursday

From: Mary Karr
Subject: **Missing plus notes. Xo**
Date: October 17, 2010 7:37:08 PM CDT
To:

SONGS

Oct 13
HUngry for home

He ate fatback on mustard greens
Ate an onion like a pear
Dipped turnips deep in morton's salt
Just a bite will take you there

Biscuits big as catcher's mitts
Use your thumb to poke one in
Fill the hole with hot cane syrup
Let it run on down your chin.

I'm hungry for home

still missing you/
1.
I heard a siren
And you came to mind
You were the pretty part of us
And I'm what's left behind
the equation's remainder
The last standing sign.
god I'm missing you

Your mouth is still soft
Your countenance fair
time stretches to shape you
Right out of thin air
But I can't hold the image
If I blink you're not there
God I'm missing you

Are you gone forever
Are you gone for good
Am I going crazy
Just wishing you would
Come round the next corner
Step offa that train
Your old black umbrella,
Face half in the rain
God I'm missing you

Listen to me breathing
Listen to me croon
If tonight you're awakened
By this sanded down moon
Cause She's simmering dim
Be gone pretty soon
God I'm missing you

You (never) ever ate fatback on mustard greens
Gobbled up an onion like a pear I mean
Dipped you a turnip deep in table salt
I don't have to tell you that it ain't your
fault
Take a biscuit bigger than catcher's mitt
Use your thumb to poke you a hole
Pour hot cane syrup down the hole amen

An open [illegible]
mean only one thing
no crumbs will [illegible]

Johnny cakes bigger than a baseball
[illegible]
Says to me there's a [illegible] up above
Angels up in heaven like to
Chow it on down
Biscuits in the oven
Makes the world go round

A [illegible] in the clouds

Or am I just crazy for thinking you would

I love fatback on mustard greens
Craving an onion like a peach
[illegible] a pot of hot collards make a mouthful out of [illegible]

Rodney Crowell
Hillbillies
December 6, 2009 11:23:55 AM CST
"mkarr

Mary Darling,
I'm not sure why I want to immortalize these people in song. So far I feel boxed in. After the wedding I'll make a sketch of the melody and mp3 it to you. Unti then, perhaps something will come to you.
R

Flatland hillbillies - Irish, Cajun, Creole mix
Daddys on an off-shore rig Sisters on a pole at slicks
Mama takes in people's washing (my brother he's a pipeline man)
We're flatland hillbillies gettin' by on what we can

Flatland hillbillies heathen to the marrowbone
Workin' on your cars drinkin' in your bars
And runnin' every redlight home

River rats and john boat shrimpers (roughneck rounders)
Rank as any wild-bull ride
Fearless as an oil-patch swamper
Waitin on a storm surge tide
God forbid we hit the lotto chances are we wind up shot
Were flatland hillbillies gettin by on what we've got

Flatland hillbillies blinded by the squad car lights
They catch you breakin' in - gets you five to ten
And you're lucky if they read you your rights

If you've never ran a trot line - never bagged an eight-point buck
Never had a squirrelmeat sammich I guess you're just out of luck
Livin' on the edge of nowhere isn't for the feint of heart
Were flatland hillbillies another other breed apart
Flatland hillbillies waitin on a war to start

Flatland Hillbillies

We're flatland hillbillies, Irish, Cajun, Creole mix
My brother's on an offshore rig, sister's on the pole at Slick's
Mama takes in people's washing, she was widowed by a pipeline man
We're flatland hillbillies getting by on what we can

We're river rats and jon boat shrimpers, trouble in our DNA
It wouldn't be the same Port Arthur if we got up and moved away
God forbid we hit the lotto, chances are we'd wind up shot
We're flatland hillbillies getting by on what we've got

Flatland hillbillies, heathen to the marrowbone
Working on your cars, drinking in your bars
And running every red light home

If you've never ran a trot line, never skinned an eight-point buck
Never had a squirrel-meat sandwich, then I guess you're just out of luck
Living on the edge of nowhere isn't for the faint of heart
We're flatland hillbillies waiting on the fire to start
Flatland hillbillies, another other breed apart

Flatland Hillbillies
Up before the break of dawn
Pall Mall at the kitchen table
Pentecostal station on
If we ever hit the lotto
Probably wouldn't change a lot
Flatland hillbillies
Getting by on what we got

Flatland Hillbillies
Crazy Cajun Creole mix
Daddy's on an offshore rig
Sister's on a pole at Slicks
Mama takes in people's washing
That makes me a pipeline man
Flatland hillbillies
Getting by on what we can.

Haw haw haw

Fat tires on my truck
And we don't give a fuck
Butt-crack hanging out my pants

Could be something in the water
Could be something in the ground
They should change the name Port Arthur
To Flatland Hillbilly Town

ERIN@ACMCOUNTRY.COM

STEVE MARKLAND

If I Could Speak to Leonard

If I could speak to Leonard I'd don my finest suit
Wind my father's pocket watch, and shine my shoes to boot
I'd learn to tie that Windsor knot I've longed so to perfect
If not to win approval, at least the man's respect
You ask me why I've come this far and what it is I seek
The answer to your question, sir, is simple yet oblique
I've come in search of pathways to the things I used to know
I'd love to speak to Leonard once before I go

If I could speak to Leonard I doubt I'd hold my own
The sixteen years he has on me, the women that he's known
His symbolism consecrates the arrow and the bow
His archer's eye sees through the sky and bends the river's flow
You ask me why I've come so far, and are my motives pure
My body longs for healing, my spirit for the cure
To put me in the state of mind that elevates the heart
I need to speak to Leonard, my time is running short

Who more than the Rabbi poet, Buddhist monk, and sage
Divines the deep and holy text in song and on the page
Be still my comprehension cries, there's so much more than this
I'd love to speak to Leonard, could you put me on the list?

If I could speak to Leonard among the things I'd say
Would not be how I love your work and that strange guitar you play
Perhaps I'd bow in silence and leave the man in peace
Content myself with what I know of Montreal and Greece

You ask me why I've come this far, by now you might have guessed
I've come here for the work at hand, I've come here for the rest
The lost soul loves a ladies' man as much as any girl
I need to speak to Leonard before I leave this world

RC & MK

VINCE GILL

Oklahoma Borderline

Well it's rainin' down in Houston, I've got holes in both my shoes
Baby's put me on the street, she says "I'm through with you"
If she thinks I'm gonna miss her, someone tell her that she's wrong
I'm goin' back to Oklahoma, boys, 'cause that's where I belong

I need one good ride, I'll be satisfied
Come on Oklahoma borderline
If we roll all night, she'll be comin' into sight
Come on Oklahoma borderline

Well, now I don't need no Texas girl doggin' me around
I may be an Okie, son, but I've still been to town
Well those Oklahoma city girls they always treat you right
Tell mama and them that I'm comin' home, I'm leavin' out tonight

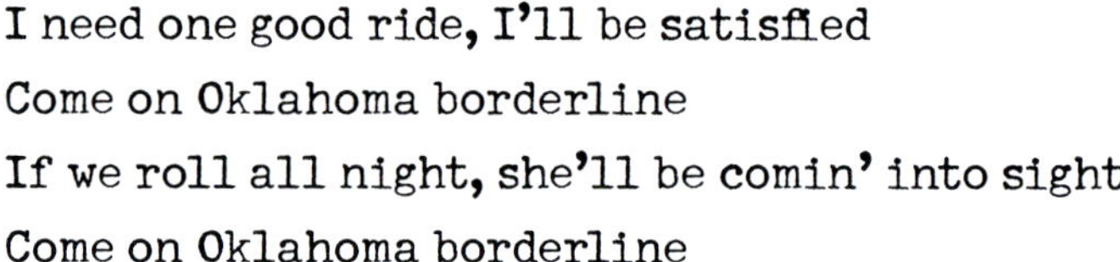

I need one good ride, I'll be satisfied
Come on Oklahoma borderline
If we roll all night, she'll be comin' into sight
Come on Oklahoma borderline

So with two bucks in my pocket and my thumb stuck in the wind
When I cross Red River, boys, I won't be back again
Give me old back roads and truck stops and 18 wheels that whine
And some good ol' boy to take me to that Oklahoma line

I need one good ride, I'll be satisfied
Come on Oklahoma borderline
If we roll all night, she'll be comin' into sight
Come on Oklahoma borderline

Vince Gill, RC & Guy Clark

It's Hard to Kiss the Lips at Night That Chew Your Ass Out All Day Long

She used to call me baby, I thought she was such a lady
My, how things have changed since time's moved on
I'd give her my last dollar but now all she'll do is holler
Oh, my life has become a country song

I've learned she can resist me by the way she always disses me
And comes to bed at night with that cold cream on
Sometimes I might feel frisky but these days it's just too risky
It's hard to kiss the lips at night that chew you ass out all day long

All day long, it goes on and on
If a tree fell in the forest and she didn't hear it, would I still be wrong?
I guess I should admit it, she ain't ever gonna quit it
It's hard to kiss the lips at night that chew you ass out all day long

(Spoken)
Man, I remember when her eyes used to be so blue and shiny
But my god, what's happened to her hiney?
Man, that thing's gotten big enough to land a small plane on
I used to roll her in the clover, thank God those days are over
It's hard to kiss the lips at night that chew you ass out all day long

All day long, she gnaws on and on
If someday they drop the big one
I'll say, sweet Jesus, she's finally gonna leave me alone
It's alright if we say it 'cause the radio won't play it
It's hard to kiss the lips at night that chew you ass out all day long
It's hard to kiss the lips at night that chew you ass out all day long

Vince Gill & RC
'04

I Hope You Shed a Million Tears

I gave my heart and soul to you, you done me wrong for years
I hope someday you suffer too and shed a million tears

Now I can see you clear as day there on our wedding night
The warm glow of your heart so gay, your eyes blue, shining bright
Your lips were like a rose red wine the stars alone can yield
My one and only valentine, my lily of the field
Then there came a stranger to our town, a man of worldly charms
Who turned our whole world upside down and stole you from my arms
Our love was like a sacred scroll you ne'er did learn to read
I gave to you my heart and soul, and you left it there to bleed

I made a vow to stand by you down through our golden years
You broke my heart and left me blue to shed a million tears

You said goodbye so casually and I took it hard, it's true
The Bible says forgive you but that's something I can't do
I loved you like there's no tomorrow and found out that there's not
Your Romeo came passing through and Cupid fired a shot
When the world was ours your heart was mine and our dreams were one of bliss
The days were like a winding stream, the nights were like a kiss
So, we stood before our savior, true believers in his grace
I gave my very soul to you and you threw it in my face

I said I'd be right there with you when we face our final years
I hope someday you suffer too and shed a million tears
Yes, I hope someday you suffer too and shed a million tears

Hank Williams (Sr.) – Rodney Crowell - Vince Gill
2011

BERNIE TAUPIN

Artificial Light

It's spooky out tonight, the desert is so quiet
Midnight lunar landscape like a ghost
I'm somewhere in between the truth and Abilene
My destination California coast

You bet I'm feeling better, you bet I feel alright
Out here taking comfort on the road tonight
I'm a long way from home, passing through the twilight zone
It ain't seldom I've seen such a welcome sight as artificial light

Hey, I could be from Mars out here underneath the stars
Pulling into last chance Texaco
There's nothing way out here but these diesel pumps and beer
And another moonlit million miles to go

You bet I'm feeling better, you bet I feel alright
Out here taking comfort on the road tonight
I'm a long way from home, passing through the twilight zone
It ain't seldom I've seen such a welcome sight as artificial light

It's limbo way out here, just some underage cashier
Another tank top sweetheart slinging gasoline
The coffee tastes like crude, some whacked out skateboard dude
Is reading *Guns & Ammo* magazine
Meanwhile, here I am, a free man on the lam
Yesterday, just one big freaking mess
Two songbirds on a wire killed by friendly fire
And who's to blame is anybody's guess

You bet I'm feeling better, you bet I feel alright
Out here taking comfort on the road tonight
I'm a long way from home, passing through the twilight zone
It ain't seldom I've seen such a welcome sight as artificial light
I'm east of Dos Cabezas headed west from Sulphur Springs
Twenty-one straight hours in a mad machine
I'm rough around the edges, I'm ragged but I'm right
The Casa Grande outskirts come into sight
And it's artificial light
Artificial light

Bernie Taupin & RC
'03

JOHN LEVENTHAL

Nobody's Gonna Tear My Playhouse Down

Don't know a dollar from a doughnut hole
Don't know tomorrow from a week ago
Don't know the reason why you skipped this town
You had me thinking you might stick around
Well, there ain't nobody gonna tear my playhouse down

I hear your name all up and down the row
I'm not ashamed to let my feelings show
Don't know the reason why you changed your tack
I do believe your ship ain't coming back
But there ain't nobody gonna tear my playhouse down

I know I act the part, a man without a heart
So, it would be a lie if I denied it's true

Some say your heart was just an open gate
And from the start it was a bad mistake
Well, there ain't nobody gonna tear my playhouse down

I know I'm acting tough to prove I'm strong enough
It would be a lie if I deny it's true

I'm gonna build a house of mud and brick
Seal the walls around me ten feet thick
Construct a shelter out of solid rock
To give me shelter from the bombs you drop
There ain't nobody gonna tear my playhouse down
No, there ain't nobody gonna tear my playhouse down

John Leventhal & RC
'92

Hymn # 43

I don't know if I'll ever find Jesus
But I can't say I won't some day
There were times when I thought I could feel it
To have it slip away
So, I'm careful about good intentions
My own and the guy's next door
Whose hell I'll pay come the judgement day
Fair warning for to sin no more

What if God sees the need for religion
As something I can't share
For to righteously judge my brother
Seems such a needless use of prayer
And this thing 'bout the pearled gates of heaven
And those that would be denied
And here we are in an endless war
With God forever on our side

Praise be the life in me, praise be the life in you
Sing, sing, let freedom ring, there will always be more work to do

As for love, I was all in a hurry
To drink the taverns dry
And the walls I built around me
To keep my hopes up high
In time I was granted a vision
Of faces as of yet unknown
And a place somewhere in the great out there
Where I don't have to die alone

Praise be the life in me, praise be the life in you
Sing, sing, let freedom ring, there will always be more work to do

RC & John Leventhal
'20

JIMMY McCARTHY

I Belong to You

When the day comes winding down and night falls at my door
I'll be coming home again for to leave your arms no more
And I will take your hand in mine and hold it with my own
Till forever comes, I promise you will never be alone

There are no rules, no walls, no lines
No guns, no gates, where real love shines
On in the land where nothing dies
And I belong to you

And I'll find in my own way the words to speak my heart
And I promise till my dying day, we will never be apart

There are no rules, no walls, no lines
No guns, no gates, where real love shines
On in the land where nothing dies
And I belong to you

There are no rules, no walls, no lines
Where I belong to you

RC & Jimmy McCarthy
'97 Clifden, Ireland

Heaven on Earth (Reasons to Leave)

Ireland's a dream of hope and what the day will bring
The land and the sea is what I've come to trust
All that I am is telling me I should not go
All that I know is they're telling me I must

Reasons to leave are money and finding better work
Reasons to stay are music and love
Reasons to leave are fortune and fame, for what it's worth
The reason to stay is Heaven on Earth

My brothers are ten and sisters I have five
Four to one bed is room enough to grow
All that we are is all that I've ever known
And all that I have will be here when I'm gone

Reasons to leave are money and finding better work
Reasons to stay are music and love
Reasons to leave are fortune and fame, for what it's worth
The reason to stay is Heaven on Earth

KIERAN GOSS

I've heard about work up in Boston
Laying track down to St. Augustine
Sometimes with an eye for New Zealand I lean

Reasons to leave are money and finding better work
Reasons to stay are music and love
Reasons to leave are fortune and fame, for what it's worth
The reason to stay is Heaven on Earth
The reason to stay is Heaven on Earth
The reason to stay is Heaven on Earth

Kieran Goss & RC
'97 Clifden, Ireland

ELEANOR McEVOY

Please Heart, You're Killing Me

Café windows, street lamps, neon lights ablaze
That shine all over town
In brilliant conversation with somebody new
He's out there making the rounds
Please heart, you're killing me

Out among the faces where a sideways glance
Says romance on a whim
Pretty boys with blue eyes smilin', stylin'
Just reminding me of him
Please heart, you're killing me

I can't go out at night, I can't stay here at home
I can't do anything because he'll be there
I can't get out of bed, I can't get any sleep
I can't have any fun because he'll be there
What does he care?

Everywhere I turn I see
The past jumps out in front of me – hello
Someone's got it in for me
This whole damned town has secrets I don't know
Please heart, you're killing me
Please heart, you're killing me

Four A.M. I brave the cold
The garbage trucks are on a roll - surprise
A vision through the subway steam
I see him and I can't believe my eyes
Please heart, you're killing me
Please heart, stop killing me

Eleanor McEvoy & RC
'97 Clifden, Ireland

I'm Alone But You're Still Here With Me

When my heart is cold and empty
And the truth my eyes can't see
And each day brings only darkness
I'm alone but you're still here with me

There was a time we were together
And our love was young and free
Now it's gone, my world has ended
I'm alone but you're still here with me

I go back to where we started
And the way things used to be
What went wrong, I keep on asking
'Cause I'm alone and you're still here with me

I just can't see the rhyme or reason
For this life of misery
Why go on, my world has ended
I'm alone but you're still here with me
Yes, I'm alone but you're still here with me

RC & Jeff Healey
'97. Clifden, Ireland

JEFF HEALEY

U Don't Know How Much I Hate U

Night after night, day after day
I pass by the house that once was my home
I look through the window, I lean on the bell
There's a light on but no sign of you
That strange looking car in the driveway tells me you're there
I know you're there
I feel like a chump bumming dimes on the street
Lowlife and useless with rags on my feet showing through

You don't know how much I hate everything about you
Your honey red lips and your eyes, big and sparkling blue
The curve of your hips and your black-Irish hair
Send a shiver that runs through and through
You don't know how much I hate you
I just wish it was true

You were kind to my mother, you were good to my friends
You were passionate, faithful and strong
I must have been sleeping, it feels like a dream
And I can't say just where I went wrong

Like a dog in the garbage with rocks in my head
I'm strung out and crazy and can't find the thread running through

You don't know how much I hate everything about you
Your voice like good bourbon, so elegant, tasteful and smooth
With a flick of a match I could burn down this house
Taking every last memory of you
You don't know how much I hate you
You don't know how much I hate you
You don't know how much I hate you
I wish it were true

RC & Steve Lukather
'98

There Lost Souls Survivin
on Hard Knocks & Vice
In a World Just as
Nasty
& your World
Is Nice
Baby Blue

this
I'm Lost In a World
Full of Hard Knocks & Vice
Lost Souls as Plenty
as

Our World is Wasted
As your World Is Nice

Like a Dog
In the Garbage
You Kicked In the
Head
I'm Strung out
& Crazy & Can't
Find the Thread
Running
Thru

Alleyways Dark Sidewalks are Bare
Time on the Streets Empty & Cold Time on my Hands
I'm Looking For Something to Knock out the Night
Till the Sun Comes up Shining Like New
The Chill In my Bones Reminds me Nobody Cares
Life ain't Fair

I'm a Dog In the Garbage Kicked In the Head
with Rocks In my Head
Strung out & Edgy
& Can't Find the Running Through
Thread
Baby Blue

I feel Like a Chump
Dumped out on the Street
Lonely & useless as
Kicked on my feet

MICHAEL McGLYNN

I'm Tied To Ya

With faith beyond religion we search the great unknown
Free fall into darkness, someplace we've never gone
I'm tied to ya, I'm tied to ya

Let's push it to the limit, as far as we can see
Till there are no walls still standing and there's only you and me
I'm tied to ya, I'm tied to ya

I can't deny that I believe these things you say are true
I've seen the way you gauge each distant star
As long as I can be myself and still be there with you
I'll go anywhere you ask me, near or far
I'm tied to ya, I'm tied to ya

Tomorrow don't mean much to me, look what we have today
Right here in this minute, babe, is where I want to stay
Tied to ya, I'm tied to ya

I've heard it said beware the fist behind your lover's kiss
And stand up guys have knocked me down before
But to rise with you above the petty politics of bliss
I'll gladly make my heart an open door

I'm tied to ya, I'm tied to ya
I'm tied to ya, I'm tied to ya
Tied to ya, tied to ya

RC & Michael McGlynn. Clifden, Ireland/Franklin, Tennessee
'97–'17

It Doesn't Hurt Right Now (But It Will Again)

(He)
It doesn't hurt right now, I can breathe again
There's change in the air, I can see and hear
It doesn't hurt right now, I can talk about it
The worst of the shame is the least of my fear

(She)
Could you ever see just you and me
Alone in this room, or does he make it three
"I'm sorry" sounds so small compared to what's true
I lied to myself when I lied to you

(He)
It doesn't hurt right now, I can hear what you have to say
I can forgive, but forget? Not yet
It doesn't hurt right now but we both know it will again
The ghosts of the past feast on regret

(She)
Needs are like rivers, you can't stop their will
A heart that goes hungry demands to be filled
I see that now, I was lonely, I took the bait
But I long to be filled by you, it's never too late

(He)
It doesn't hurt right now, so what does that say about me?
I learned to be numb a long time ago, to soften the blow
It doesn't hurt right now (I hurt right now)
I don't know what you want from me (Why won't you give it to me?)
I moved out of my heart a long time ago

Jewel & RC

Don't Think That I Can't Feel You When You're Gone

Your kiss goodbye a whisper on my cheek
One breath away from I can't even speak
Your voice alive inside my chain of bones
Don't think that I can't feel you when you're gone

Your leg against my leg while you're asleep
A whole world undercover, ours to keep
These buried treasures I keep stumbling on
Don't think that I can't feel you when you're gone

> These are the things that I
> Will use to just get by till you get home
> These are the things that make it easier to take
> The time alone, it's only time alone

Your perfume on the collar of my shirt
So sweet and faint it almost makes me hurt
Your goodbye glance that keeps me going strong
Don't think that I can't feel you when you're gone

> These are the things that you
> And you alone can do to keep me here
> These little things in life you use to dull the knife
> And make it clear there's nothing here to fear

Everything about you is so defined
I know you like the back of my own mind
You're a dream that I can put my finger on
Don't think that I can't feel you when you're gone
No, don't think that I can't feel you when you're gone

John Paul White & RC

KEITH URBAN

You Won

There was a world outside my door
I wasn't in touch with anymore
There was a way I used to feel
I knew what was and was not real

You built a bridge, I tore it down
I felt safe on shaky ground
I was a master of despair
Making believe I didn't care

I shouldn't be standing here today
After all the crazy things I've done
I'm ready to fall and that's okay
I ran as far as I could run
You won

Out of a world turned upside down
It took some time to come around
Out of a dream you made me whole
You built a fire down in my soul

I shouldn't be standing here today
After all the crazy things I've done
I'm ready to fall and that's okay
I ran as far as I could run
You won

Keith Urban & RC

Rodney Crowell

The Border

I work on the border, I see what I see
I work on the border and it's workin' on me
I lie awake at night knowing what I know
There's a price on the head of every border patrol
Where the smugglers do business, that's where I make a stand
I know this old desert like the back of my hand
I see greed in the bushes, I see snakes in the dark
Some are friends of my brothers, can't you hear them dogs bark?

I come home to Maria at the end of that day
In the shape of a shadow, holding demons at bay
"It's just the border," they say

It was Mexican soldiers out of a black Humvee
With their guns to their shoulders aimed at my partner and me
Ah, they drove away laughing but the message was clear
We don't care about nothing but the money down here

I come home to Maria in a bulletproof vest
With the weight of the whole wide world bearing down on my chest
It's just the border, I guess

From the shacks and the shanties come the hungry and poor
Some to drown at the crossing, some to suffer no more

I guess you heard about Ramos and Compean
Both of 'em friends of mine, both good men
They did one right thing and look what they got
Federal prison where they're both gonna rot

I come home to Maria, where else would I go?
Across the river to die by myself down in old Mexico
It's just the border, you know

Allen Shamblin & RC
'06–'18

Open Season on My Heart

JAMES SLATER

Here's to the corners yet to turn
Here's to the bridges yet to burn
Here's to the whole thing blown apart
It's open season on my heart

Days go by like flying bricks
Leave gaping holes too deep to fix
I'd just stay home if I were smart
It's open season on my heart

I can't blame anyone but me
For this reckless fool I've come to be
My tired excuses just don't fit
Things don't look good from where I sit

I've tried to change without much luck
I reach the point where I get stuck
I hit the streets, the fireworks start
It's open season on my heart

I can't be something that I'm not
Can't give you what I haven't got
I don't know where or why or when
I only know the shape I'm in

Here's to the clown down in the mouth
Here's to the whole thing going south
My one true love turned poison dart
It's open season on my heart

I'd just stay home if I were smart
It's open season on my heart

RC & James Slater

Lynn Goldsmith

You're Only Happy When You're Miserable

Go sell your snake oil to someone you used to know
I've heard your whining 'til my motor just won't go
The sky ain't falling though, I know you wish it would
I almost hate to tell you that I'm leaving you for good
You're only happy when you're miserable
I'm all amped up, you're all clamped down
I've never seen you with a cup half full
Worst case scenario, yeah, that's the girl I know
You're only happy when you're miserable

Go tell your mother it was all my fault
Your baby brother I ain't worth my salt
Your bold prediction that I'd bail on you
Turns out my nightmare is your dream come true
You're only happy when you're miserable
Go on and run it in the ground
It's high time I get it through my own thick skull
Your doomsday fantasy means more to you than me
You're only happy when you're miserable

Don't know the last time that I've seen you smile
I only know it's been a long, long while
I tried to change you like I thought I should
You pulled the wool on me, it ain't no mystery

You court disaster with a surgeon's skill
I've got good news for you I've had my fill
The sun is shining and you're pulling out your hair
Too close to crazy to pretend I even care
You're only happy when you're miserable
I ramp it up, you clamp it down
You've made an art form out of pitiful
It's raining cats and dogs, you'd rather snakes and frogs
You're only happy when you're miserable

RC & Erin Enderlin

ERIN
ENDERLIN

Sweet Lucinda, look out your window
LA freeway just like the man said
People honking their horns and pointing guns at your head, sweet Lucinda
In the land of cotton you're not forgotten
Mississippi River just rolls on through
Everybody's wondering what happened to you in the land of cotton
Down on the Delta, remember your soul
We're waiting just to welcome you back to the fold
Tomorrow comes early, you better get humming
The whole damn town is gonna know that you're coming

Bring it on home to Memphis
Bring it on home and give us a thrill
Bring it on home and send me the bill
Bring it on home to Memphis

Beale Street was jumping the day you were born
WC Handy was blowing his horn
From the bluffs to Mud Island the music grew quiet
"Mystery Train" put a hush on the night
Fireflies made light of the hot summer breeze
The wind was a whisper through the tops of the trees
Rain started falling, river grew lazy
Bring it on home you're making me crazy

We've got hot buttered biscuits and dewberry pie
White flour gravy in an endless supply
Cucumber salad right out of the ground
And cold soda water just to wash it all down
Down on the Delta where cotton is king
We only want to treat you like a homecoming queen
Tomorrow comes early, it's never too late
The whole damned town's gonna open the gate

Bring it on home to Memphis
Bring it on home and that'll be good
Bring it on home to the old neighborhood
Bring it on home to Memphis

RC & Larry Klein

I grew up lean if you know what I mean, and it ain't my scene to come on green
I know the way the world goes 'round without a question
I've slept with queens, I've dined with slaves, St Petersburg to Santa Fe
Lucky sevens all the way without exception
I've rolled in dough with friend and foe, caught cocktail talk where no one walks
And I hung the moon too soon to be respected
I've played the pups, I've spun the wheel, I'll tell you exactly how I feel
Never say you're sorry, just be careful

Just a little place called lonely, ma'am
That's where I've been, that's where I am
There ain't no gold and there ain't no sidewalk Sunday
It's just a little place called lonely, man
Make no mistake about what I can
I should be Hollywood on wheels but I'm on fire

On a cowboy bus in a New York zoo
I only did what I had to do
I pulled a gun and took the money with me
The law cut me off but it ain't no loss
I figure I'm the boss no matter what the cost
I don't take no to be the answer to one of my questions
So, I rode my Harley into the ground
I laid her down without a sound
And I knew right then and there y'all would not miss me

It's just a little place called lonely, ma'am
That's where I've been, that's where I am
There ain't no gold and there ain't no sidewalk Sunday
It's just a little place called lonely, man
Make no mistake about what I can
I could be Hollywood on wheels but I'm on fire
Each and every day is Monday blue
You hold your own, that's just what you do
And if any day the sun comes through it ain't tomorrow

EMORY GORDY

Tell Fast Eddie and the Electric Japs
On their surface trip I checked it out
He's a money man, it's a funny world, and I'll be watching
I want to tell you just one more thing
And I hope it don't cause no one no rain
But there's a window up above and it ain't no George Jones song . . . Baby!

RC & Emory Gordy
'80

(in memory of Peter Sheridan)

When Losers Rule the World

When losers rule the world, I'm the man who would be king
When losers rule the world, I'll be in songs that children sing
That tell the tale of how I fell when I lost everything
When losers rule the world

When losers rule the world, they'll salute when I walk by
When losers rule the world, they'll applaud each time I cry
The tears that fall will make men all feel humbled at my side
When losers rule the world

> My time in the sun will surely come
> And a million eyes will see
> What you've done to me
> When losers rule the world

When losers rule the world, I'll be a big-shot then
When losers rule the world, I'll be a prince among men
I'll lift my glass to the past that made me what I am
When losers rule the world
When losers rule the world

Ben Vaughan & RC
'90

United Artists Music Publishing Group

All you have to do is tell the truth pain & all
Music takes away the layers of protection
No moment is stilled in music like the earth it changes
All you have to do is tell the truth
When youre down to nothing music tells your story
When youre up to everything music tells your story
Were really all just alike its our fear of being the same
That makes us different. Thank God for human beings.

Susanna Clark

Soul is a four letter word

Wait a Minute

Wait a minute, hey, just a minute
I just need a little time
I can get myself together, give me half a chance
Baby, to collect my mind
Wait a minute, hey, just a minute
I need a little room to breathe
Slow down, slow down, we can turn it around
Baby, you don't have to leave

I just want to call a time out, baby
Things are moving way too fast
I've been having trouble keeping up with you
I don't think I'm gonna last
I love you like there's no tomorrow
But I've got to make it through today
So, have a little patience with the shape I'm in
You don't have to throw it all away

Wait a minute, hey, just a minute
I just need a little time
I can get myself together, give me half a chance
Baby, to collect my mind
Wait a minute, hey, just a minute
I need a little room to breathe
Slow down, slow down, we can turn it around
Baby, you don't have to leave

Everything about this love we share is something that I can't explain
Every time I think I'll get somewhere the rug comes out from under and I'm going down the drain

Wait a minute, hey, just a minute
I just need a little time
I can get myself together, give me half a chance
Baby, to collect my mind
Wait a minute, hey, just a minute
I need a little room to breathe
Slow down, slow down, we can turn it around
Baby, you don't have to leave
Slow down, slow down, we can turn it around
Baby, you don't have to leave

RC & Hank DeVito

RICHARD DOBSON

Deep in the Heart of Uncertain Texas

The crickets are singing, the blue gills are biting
The fireflies are flashing with all of their might
Just forty-odd mile from the Rio Palm Isle
The whole gang's gone fishing on a full moonlit night

We get high on the lake and we float down the river
Get off on the back roads, get lost in the woods
Very deep in the heart of Uncertain, Texas
I've tried hard to leave here but never did could

Tomorrow we'll have us the world's largest fish fry
Eat catfish and crappie till they come out our ears
Have it made in the shade of a sleepy pine thicket
Get covered up in chiggers and drink ten tubs of beer

We get high on the lake and we float down the river
Get off on the back roads, get lost in the woods
Very deep in the heart of Uncertain, Texas
I've tried hard to leave here but never did could

Give me a guitar and a long-legged girl
A dime bag of dirt weed and a six-pack of Pearl
Take 59 Highway 'cross the Cass county line
That's where you'll find me way back in the pine

RC & Richard Dobson
'76–'18

Dear Rodney,

Goddamn it, I wish Mickey Newbury was alive to hear your version of his favorite of my songs. You kicked ass, son. And thanks for the slight line change ("Where she lay down on my bed.") All the difference in the world, and its the way I'll sing it from now on.

Tribute Albums scare the hell out of me, but I love this one. The soul of the songs was nailed, and I'm really honored that you're part of it. And I can't help singing harmony with you.

Peace,

Kris

Kristofferson Hana, Hawaii

Taking Flight

We were somewhere east of Hattiesburg on a lonely stretch of nightmare
Gas gauge screaming, empty headlights in a fog
Two refugees from Greenville in line to wind up roadkill
With a parakeet named Chester and a one-eyed spotted dog

We'd been plowing through each day like so much Mississippi red dirt
Burning with no purpose, save get out while we still can
Hell-bent past the point of no return and going nowhere
With the best of good intentions one more line drawn in the sand

Taking flight, forget about the landing
Wrong or right, any somewhere says it all
Taking flight, we'll be there when we get there
Next time hell starts freezing over we'll be sure to give a call

So we got our education in the arms of sweet temptation
We earned our reputation turning heartache into song
Riding high on one wing and a foxhole prayer might get you there
But that ten won't get you twenty if you bet your money wrong

Taking flight, forget about tomorrow
Wrong or right, the chips are gonna fall
Taking flight, going nowhere till we get there
Next time hell starts freezing over we'll be sure to give a call

RC & Ashley McBryde

I'll Love You Till the Day I Die

I only saw you once, it was a long, long time ago
You probably don't remember me but I thought I'd let you know
That one short conversation is still the reason why
I'll love you till the day I die

You knew I was an honest man, I guess I knew it too
But If I'd known then what I know now, I'd trade it all for you
And when you turned and walked away, I didn't bat an eye
But I'll love you till the day I die

I didn't know my heart back then, what was there to know?
If I could do it all again, I'd never let you go
Thirty minutes thirty years ago is still the reason why
I'll love you till the day I die

In case I still might sleep with you in some sweet by and by
I'm gonna love you till the day I die

RC & Chris Stapleton

CLEMENT'S LAMENT

The night before this Christmas day we'll gather 'round the tree
And sing our favorite carols filled with sentimental glee
We'll tell the same old stories so well-honed year after year
We won't bother with the truth when those we love are near

Peace, peace, peace on earth, good will to one and all
The season starts in August now, we'll see you in the mall

RC

CHRISTMAS SONGS

Jack Spencer

Christmas Everywhere

Christmas, Christmas, Christmas, Christmas, Christmas everywhere
Christmas, Christmas, Christmas, Christmas, pulling out my hair
Shoppers lined up out the door, traffic backed up miles or more
It's Christmastime so what the heck, let's go spend the whole paycheck

Christmas, Christmas, Christmas, Christmas, morning, noon and night
Christmas, Christmas, Christmas, Christmas, Christmas, am I right?
Larry wants a Lincoln Log, Carrie wants a puppy dog
Johnny wants a ball and bat, let's make that a cowboy hat
Mama wants the kitchen sink, daddy wants a stiffer drink
Grandma wants to cut the crap, Grandpa wants a nice long nap

Christmas, Christmas, Christmas, Christmas, Christmas out the waz
Christmas, Christmas, Christmas, Christmas, Christmas up the schnoz
Come all ye faithful, don't be slow, it's Christmas time, you can't say no

Rudy wants a motor boat, Judy wants a new mink coat
Benny wants a brand-new car, Jenny wants to be a star
Billy wants the state of Texas, Lilly wants to sue her exes
Maggie wants a string of pearls, Donald wants to rule the world

Christmas, Christmas, Christmas, Christmas, Christmas here again
Christmas, Christmas, Christmas, Christmas, Christmas wearing thin
Deck the halls, 'tis the season, we don't need no rhyme or reason
It's Christmas time, go spread the cheer, pretty soon it'll be next year

As long as I'm up on your knee
Please, Santa, won't you bring to me
A time machine that I can ride
Back to the day John Lennon died
I know that I could stop the man
Who held that pistol in his hand
And by the way, for what it's worth
Please bring my sister peace on earth

Christmas, Christmas, Christmas, Christmas, Christmas makes me happy
I love Christmas cold and grey, I love it sweet and sappy
Says crazy kissing cousin Flo, "Let's break out the mistletoe"
Spike the punch with something strong, sing our favorite Christmas song
Up on the rooftop, click, click, click, that wee spry elf they call St. Nick

RC & John Jorgenson

Christmas Makes Me Sad

Christmas makes me sad
Christmas makes me blue
Christmas makes me lonely without you

I wander down these city streets
It seems like everyone I meet is happy
'Cause it's Christmas time
But something else hangs on my mind
The sights and sounds 'round this old town
Says it's that time of year but you're not here
And I'll spend my silent night alone

Christmas makes me sad
Christmas makes me blue
Christmas makes me lonely without you

It wasn't very long ago
We made angels in the snow
A winter's wonderland of dreams
Isn't always what it seems
A million points of light so bright
Says something in the air but I don't care
I'll spend my silent night alone

Christmas makes me sad
Christmas makes me blue
Christmas makes me lonely without you

Chuck Cannon & RC

Merry Christmas from an Empty Bed

That artificial Christmas tree my baby left behind
I told her when she brought it home it suited me just fine
I can't believe one little lie still haunts me to this day
But what else can I say, she's the one that got away

The evergreen seems pointless for a tired old fool like me
The fake one more resembles now the man I've come to be
And, anyway, the slowly-turning colors of the wheel
Reminds me how I feel, this really can't be real

Red, yellow, green
Green, yellow, red
Merry Christmas from an empty bed

Outside my window all the streets are covered up with snow
Somehow, I thought believing in our love would make it grow
God knows faith can cover up a multitude of sins
But you wouldn't let me in and I trim the tree again

In red, yellow, green
Green, yellow, red
Merry Christmas from an empty bed

So, she learned to read my lies like tea leaves in a cup
And here it is that time of year to put that thing back up
I guess I've grown accustomed to the artificial glow
And now she'll never know how much I loved her so

Red, yellow, green
Green, yellow, red
Merry Christmas from an empty bed

RC & Brennen Leigh

Christmas in Vidor

Christmas in Vidor, 88 degrees
The taco stand's padlocked, Spanish moss hanging from the trees
Flip-flops sticking to an asphalt road
The whole damn town decorated to implode
The lawnmower dies with a cough and a moan
Ain't nothing 'round here you'd want to stick a bow on

How'd I wind up down here, you might ask?
For that story, brother, you're gonna' have to pony up cash
I planned to leave with a man dressed up like the president
But he got him a union card and we never went
Pipe fittin' wasn't no fun
So he got him a bass boat and he got him a gun
He got me a duplex and he got me some kids
We were gonna go to AstroWorld but we never did

Christmas in Vidor, ain't it a bitch
Christmas in Vidor, give me the red bug itch
Christmas in Vidor, that's ash, that ain't snow
Christmas in Vidor, nowhere to go

Won't build no snowman, won't drink no nog
Just wonder around in a bayou fog
Take out the turkey, lay down the grub
Fix my face, do the dishes, throw the kids in the tub
Spend the late night standing inside the fridge door
Bathed in the green light and hungry for more
The back door's wide open but here's what I know
The end of the driveway is as far as I'll go

Christmas in Vidor, leave me alone
Christmas in Vidor, just being here's gone
Christmas in Vidor, can't pay the bills
Christmas in Vidor, pop a few pills
Christmas in Vidor, our baby girl's due
Christmas in Vidor, hope it don't look like you

I'll wear the school colors, I'll go to the game
I'll take the prom pictures, don't they all look the same?
Come Christmas in Vidor this time next year
I'll be hopped up and propped up on Prozac and beer

RC & Mary Karr

Let's Skip Christmas This Year

Let's skip Christmas this year, Mary, what do you say?
Can't we just let it slide like it was any old day?
What, with the money we'd save, we can just disappear
Before we both die of cheer, let's skip Christmas this year

We'll stay out of the mall, all the glom and the haste
Just not deck the halls or stuff food in our face

We'll tell our family and friends that we still love 'em a ton
But we've just taken ill and we won't be much fun
Oh, no, don't send us a thing, we're contagious we fear
Can't you imagine their sneer if we skip Christmas this year?

We may share DNA but we're not the same kind
Let 'em bicker and fuss, let 'em drink themselves blind

Let's skip Christmas this year, can't we sit this one out?
Just pretend we don't know what the fuss is about
Dinner plates will be thrown and your drunk uncle will leer
We don't belong in that sphere, lets skip Christmas this year

Before we both die of cheer let's skip Christmas this year

RC & Mary Karr

Christmas in New York

That Christmas in New York, Mayflower Hotel
When first we got together I didn't know you well
With popcorn and paper, we trimmed us a tree
That Christmas in New York when it was just you and me
Oh, what a night, oh, what a day

That Christmas in LA, Santa Ana winds
Drunk and disorder was the shape we'd gotten in
Eat, drink and be merry, tomorrow you'll cry
When it's Christmas in LA, let sleeping dogs lie
Some other night, some other day

The thing that I could never quite put my finger on
Before we both got started, it was already gone
Was it something in our nature that kept us looking for the worst?
Only three feet from the well and we'd both rather die of thirst

There's one thing I can count on but never understand
The way that I remember you, I'd do it all again
In spite of burned out bridges we can't get back across
There's something at the heart of what we had I've never lost

It's Christmas in New York and wouldn't you know
Gramercy Park Hotel and a half foot of snow
It's your kind of weather, that time of year
It's Christmas in New York, I wish you were here
Just for one night, just for one day
Just for one night, just for one day

Come Christmas

Christmas makes me stop and wonder where you are
Just like every other day I've seen so far
To make believe this Christmas Eve that you'll come home
No more to roam is madness I can't let myself go near

'Tis the season now that always gives me pause
And not because I don't believe in Santa Claus
Ornaments and stockings hung without much care
If you're out there, it's just the way to end another year
Come Christmas day, hope you're okay
Come Christmas night, hope you're alright
Not knowing is the hardest part of all

To deck these halls with holly boughs and mistletoe
Seem so much in denial of the truth we know
You've hurt yourself in ways that can't be understood
It can't feel good
Pray tell explain why this might bring good cheer
Can I just say I wish that you were here?

Come Christmas day, hope you're okay
Come Christmas night, hope you're alright
Not knowing is the hardest part of all

RC - Addie Brue & Iris Brue

Christmas for the Blues

I haven't seen you 'round here since I don't know when
Makes me stop and wonder just how long it's been
The sight of you says nothing but good news
You look like a Christmas for the blues

Seeing you reminds me of the way we were
Just standing here beside you makes the feeling stir
I can't deny your leaving left a bruise
You look like a Christmas for the blues

I don't have to ask if things are going well
As for me, well, let's just say there's not that much to tell

Once upon a time back when the world was young
With you I really thought I'd found the ladder's rung
In life we learn to live and love and lose
You look like a Christmas for the blues

Everything about you says you're doing fine
I don't have to ask you if the years have all been kind

I hate to say goodbye, I hope I see you 'round
Maybe when the season starts to wind back down
I'll surely understand should you refuse
But you look like a Christmas for the blues

CAA

STUDIO

KEEP

GET THE

ON BAR 64

TOGETHER

QUIT

P.S.

EMPTY

THE

BOTTLE

DOES

Keep

ALBUM CUTS

The Ballad of Artemis and Orion

Artemis was her father's daughter, she wore the old man down
Willed herself down off the mount and searched the whole world 'round
She wandered through the forest's dark, a light to her own kind
And what she learned from leaving home is nothing stays behind

She sought the ways of wisdom in the solitude she kept
And swore no man could claim her from the dirt bed where she slept
She who seeks the highest truth has done so from the start
And those who wish to know themselves must follow their own heart

A hundred trillion years could pass and still the stars could shine
Or be gone in sixty seconds if someday they change their mind
It's late out in the future and the past is in a huff
The journey in and of itself has never been enough

Orion had charisma and he smelled like human waste
Goat tartare and bone meal were the staples of his taste
His beard was black and flaming, his eyes were bloody red
His arrows flew like birds of prey, he was a god they said

Sirius was the dog that made all other dogs look tame
Allegiance to your master was his mother's maiden name
Orion took his faithful friend forever as his own
Together they went off in search of goat and marrow bone

Artemis and Orion weren't a match made in the sky
He wandered into her world with a patch over his eye
He kicked her dog, spooked her horse and killed her goats galore
Raped her without passion and proceeded hence to snore

Artemis lay there thinking that she might as well be dead
She killed him without blinking with a scorpion instead
She buried him beside the sea beneath a mossy mound
And news of what had come to be was quickly spread around

Orion did some hard time in the lower rungs of hell
Until the gods took pity and put up his cosmic bail
He took his place among the stars of winter, summer, spring
But not so come November when the Scorpio is king

A hundred trillion years could pass and still the stars could shine
Or be gone in sixty seconds if someday they change their mind
It's late out in the future and the past is looking rough
The journey in and of itself has never been enough

Moving Work of Art

Time is jammed and flying fast
Brakes are bad, the potholes rough
I'm out here running from the past
What we had was not enough
I heard she just touched down in Hollywood
Her friends all say she's looking good
I saw it coming from the start
She's a moving work of art

The night is thick, the moon rings red
And the stars are out of place
My mind is liquid in my head
Beneath the waves I see her face
I'll bet she pulls herself some tall coin down
Turning heads out there in Tinsel Town
She's so cool it breaks your heart
She's a moving work of art

Who we were and what we had
Keeps me guessing to this day
It's enough to drive you mad
She's a million miles away
I'll bet she's out there thinking on her feet
Making passes thrown fall incomplete
She's as smooth as she is smart
She's a moving work of art
Do you see how she sets herself apart?
She's a moving work of art

Forgive Me, Annabelle

Maybe I was out of line, mostly I was out of touch
You lean on anger like a crutch, you're bound to take a fall
No doubt I was slow to learn, I just couldn't get the gist
So, I doubled up my fist and I punched me the wall

When you walked out on me I took the hit in stride, I'm better off, I lied
The truth may show I stood the blow but we both know
How far from grace I fell . . . forgive me, Annabelle

Who'd have thought that peace of mind would find me in the end
Nearly ten years on the mend and no getting over you
But now I'm resolute, I've seen evidence of change
At first I thought it strange and not worth clinging to

Let's set the record straight, I came around too late
Though I got there in the end, I never was your friend

When you walked out on me it tore my heart in half, and I hid behind a laugh
As I became a slave to shame I cursed your name
God damn, you rot in hell . . . can you forgive me, Annabelle?

10 Names

They were young men imprisoned on the H-blocks at Long Kesh
Interned on suspicion, doing time on remand
Republican army, some sixth generation
Something Miss Thatcher could not understand
So, the great politician took a hard stand on terror
And who 'er could blame her but the thing she'd omit
That for three-hundred years they'd been there uninvited
And the poor Catholic rabble would not idly sit

On the hard-blanket protest of '76
Four years they lived naked in a Union Jack sty
While the Queen's bitter warders kicked them and beat them
With an orange-fisted fury come the 12th of July
All bloodied and broken and in the winter-time freezing
In the summertime maggots and a shite-covered stench
But political status would not be forthcoming
For the dear Mrs. Thatcher would not give an inch

> If you're ever in Derry take a walk on the Bogside
> Where the high price of freedom stands tall
> On the Falls Road in Belfast, slow down when you ride past
> Ten names on the side of a high-gabled wall

When the hunger strike started they were men without names
Bobby Sands was the first to be heard on the street
While starving in jail he was duly elected
Member of Parliament, South Fermanagh seat
So, with things looking up, soon their spirits were lifted
In belief that her majesty soon surely must cave
But in 66 days Bobby Sands was a martyr
And nine more would follow his path to the grave

> If you're ever in Derry take a walk on the Bogside
> Where the high price of freedom stands tall
> On the Falls Road in Belfast, slow down when you ride past
> Ten names on the side of a high-gabled wall

When the hunger for justice spans eight-hundred years
It's hard to stay civil face down in the bog
Whether up from the ghetto or down the Mourne Mountains
Seems they'd rather die hungry than live like a dog

If you're ever in Derry take a walk on the Bogside
Where the high price of freedom stands tall
On the Falls Road in Belfast, slow down when you ride past
Ten names on the side of a high-gabled wall

Derry '03

When the War is Over

I need to laugh but I can't laugh
Silence is the key, they say, to make it through each endless day
So, I can't laugh
I need to cry but I can't cry
More than a year we've lived in fear but teardrops have no place in here
So, I can't cry
When the war is over we'll breathe the air again, but how long until then?
The grown-ups say it could be any day

I want to dance but I can't dance
The walls are thin, no light gets in
Day out, day in, our lives depend on a creaking floor
I want to be free but I'm not free
To ride my bike down the Prinsengracht
I could get shot but, oh, why not
I can't take it anymore
When the war is over we'll all go home again
But how long until then we dare not say it could be any day

Imprisoned in a room the same as any tomb
Behind a bookcase there's a crawlspace up a stairway to the annex
Where we pray no one suspects
That there are kind Dutch gentiles hiding German Jews

I want to be brave but I'm not brave
They came today, someone gave us away, and it's safe to say
It's cattle cars and death camps from now on
I need to be strong but I'm not strong
The raging typhus I can take, it's the racist hatred that drove the stake
Now my will to live is gone
When the war is over, will I believe again?
But how long until then?
Till we find a way this is where we stay

Amsterdam '15

I need to laugh but I can't laugh
Silence is the key they say to make it through each
Endless day I have my dreams but that's ok
I trust my fathers plan my spirit's grown numb
I need to cry but I can't cry
To shed a tear in hiding here [illegible]
I'll persevere
I'll do the best I can This much [illegible]
The tears I'll shed are in my heart
Teardrops have no place in here
[illegible] I'll face the fear
You hide your fear
The time for fear is not yet here
The time for tears has no place here
You hide your fear and follow [illegible] plan
Trust my
Pray for help to come

Oh, King Richard

Oh, King Richard, you rum runner's dream
The swiftest of outlaws I've ever seen
Your checkered flag waving so high in esteem
Till no one can catch you at all

What can you say about the man built for speed?
The master mechanic gave you what you need
Survival on instinct, a heart that don't bleed
The winning tradition of a vanishing breed

When I think about a lesser man much like myself
Alive in a vacuum, alone on a shelf
Compelled to go no place till all I've got left
Is staring at these lonely walls

Oh, King Richard, just keep up the pace
Your boot in the gas tank, your smile on your face
You set the standard that time can't erase
And God only knows how you feel

If there's life in the fast lane, you wrote the book
But it don't come as easy as you make it look
'Cause a man and his sunshades can't ever slow down
Without somebody sneakin' 'round stealing your crown

From the dirt tracks in Charlotte to the Daytona line
Your life flying by you, you don't even mind
The world loves a winner and you showed 'em all
How easy the King gets it done

Oh, King Richard, just look out below
Some punk on your bumper and you start running slow
One day you're older, next thing you know
Your races are already run
Oh, King Richard, they're trying to ditch ya
Ah, but they never can git 'cha
Man, you know how to drive like the King

Oh, King Richard, nobody can catch ya
So, they'll never forget 'cha
Man, you know how to drive like a king

Brown & Root, Brown & Root

Lord, I worked my hands in wet cement
For the county highway crew
I'm the middle boy from a family of ten
And poor sons-a-bitches were we
Pa was mean when he drank, and he always drank
And he never said three words to me

Whoo ha
Whoo ha

Lord it's hell when you're down, don't no one care
It all looks like uphill down there
'Cause you work and you climb and you smell like dirt
And you know you ain't going nowhere
At Brown & Root, Brown & Root

Whoo ha
Whoo ha

Lord the rain would come and the roof would leak
And the gas company cut off the heat
'Cause when it rains you don't work which means no pay
Which always meant not much to eat
There are too many ways to get beat
At Brown & Root, Brown & Root

'76

I'm Looking Forward to the Past

There's a girl I used to know about three broken hearts ago
I married her and left her in the dark
Vicksburg has her now and I'm headed there somehow
For to see if I can kindle that old spark
She had that Louisiana sizzle
She had that sleepy Southern sass
I split the blanket down the middle
Since then it's all been downhill fast
I'm looking forward to the past

I'm a Mississippi man and a Conway Twitty fan
And I haven't heard a song I like in years
I drive a pulpwood truck, I make an honest buck
And I'll be ready when my savior reappears
You want to think I'm dumb and lazy
Judge me entirely without class
But if you knew how Momma raised me
You'd know it's you who comes off crass
I'm looking forward to the past

He who lives and learns can't renegotiate the terms
On a freakin' frackin' future full of carbon copy crap
The stakes are through the roof but there's very little proof
That we can find fresh food and water somewhere out there off the map

I cut my teeth on hurt and I've slung my share of dirt
But I can't blame myself for everything gone wrong
What's done is done they say, if there's hell we have to pay
I might admit I must've known it all along
I don't know two nickels from a quarter
Don't know my shirttail from my ass
A modern world so out of order
We don't know how long it can last
I'm looking forward to the past

Oh, Miss Claudia

Oh, Miss Claudia
You sure been good for me
I don't birddog other women
I don't drink till I can't see

Oh, Miss Claudia
You done turned me on a light
I'm a different man forever
Since you give me back my sight

Someone said somebody said
"To thine own self be true"
Before I found you, Miss Claudia
That weren't no easy thing to do
Lawdy, Lawdy, Lawd, Miss Claudia
I waited my whole life for you
If you ever think 'bout leaving here
I'm gon' come go with you too

You paint such a pretty picture
Hanging sheets out on the line
You're the reason for the tingling
Running up and down my spine
Lawdy, Lawdy, Lawd, Miss Claudia
How come you took so long to find?
The thought of ever leaving you here
Is the last thing on my mind

Whoa, Miss Claudia
You done changed me inside out
I'm a different man forever
This there ain't no doubt about

Yeah, yeah, yeah

Famous Last Words of a Fool

Take my coat, take my hat, take my breath away just like that
Turn the tables on me, hang new labels on me
Wind the clock back nice and slow

Make me laugh till I weep, make me lonesome for you in my sleep
Is it love or lust, bottom tier or upper crust?
We'll find out soon enough, you know

Younger woman, older man
Can we make this work?
Don't you know we can
Famous last words of a fool in love

I've been out of touch so long
Been going at it hammer and tong
Sure that I could build a wall
Higher than a man can fall
Famous last words of a fool in love

This is not about a chance you take and it's not about a choice you make
Looking for the next cheap thrill or the magic in a little blue pill
This is how does it feel with your hopes up high

I might have been a handsome lad back when I didn't look so mad
But this is what I find amazing you and I could go out blazing
Famous last words of a fool in love
Famous last words of a fool

PSYCHIC

LOVE
MARRIAGE
LIFE COACH
PAST PRESENT FUTURE
HEALTH
BUSINESS

Fate's Right Hand

Cool as a rule you don't learn in no school
You don't brown nose the teacher from a dunce-hat stool
It's the hum and the rhythm of the birds and the bees
The mommas and the poppas and the monkeys in the trees
To the brothers and the sisters living life on the street
Play the hunch, pull the punch and you'll never get beat
By the junk food tattooed white dude true blued
Honky with an attitude coming unglued
Fate's right hand? I don't understand at all!

Billy Clinton loves women like a junky loves dope
Given just enough rope and the monkey gon' choke
She's a Bill Blass combo, maxed-out mombo
DKNY caught him in a lie
Ken Starr, word, man you're talking absurd
Spending forty million dollars just to give the man the bird
He's a king, she's a queen, so the rap won't stick
Get it on with a rubber and you won't get sick
Fate's right hand? I don't understand at all!

Redrum, dot com, dim sum, smart bombs
Double cappuccino and my heart's like a tom tom
Ozone long gone, that's it, I quit
Natural inclination says enough of this
Brat pack, blackjack, heart attack, crack
We need another news channel like a hole in the back
There's a 187 on the 405
And we all go to heaven on a hard disk drive
Fate's right hand? I don't understand at all!

Hard rain, fish seine, Hurricane Jane
Don't forget about Carla when you're thinking about poon-tang
Slow song, on-the-bone, rec-hall dance
Double date Debbie with a pole in your pants
First comes love like it always did
Or we wouldn't be talkin' 'bout the Houston kid
Podunk, piss chunk, old, dead, skunk drunk
Trot line Freddie's got his dogs in the trunk
Fate's right hand? I don't understand at all!

'00- Laurel Ridge

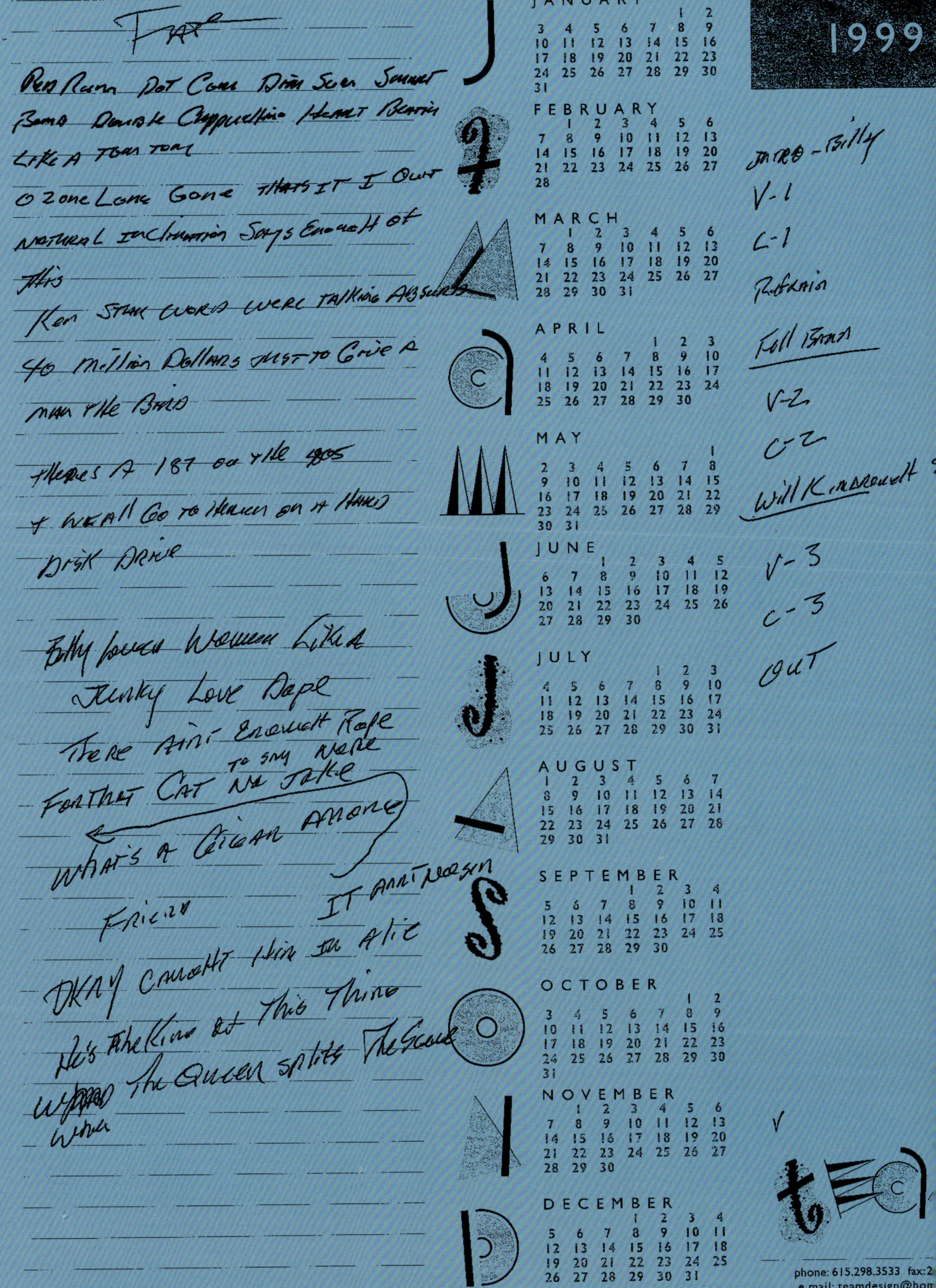

Red Rum Dot Com Brain Scan Sunset
Bomb Double Cappuccino Heart Beatin
Like a Tom Tom
Ozone Long Gone That's it I Quit
Natural Inclination Says Enough of
This
Ken Starr Word Were Talking Absurd
40 Million Dollars Just to Give a
man the Bird
There's a 187 on the 405
& We All Go to Heaven on a Hard
Disk Drive
Billy Loves Women Like a
Junky Love Dope
There Ain't Enough Rope
For That Cat to say Nope
What's a Cigar Amore
Friend
It Ain't Treason
Okay Caught Him in a Lie
He's the King of This Thing
When The Queen splits The Scene
Intro - Billy
V-1
C-1
Refrain
Full Band
V-2
C-2
V-3
C-3
Out
1999
JANUARY
FEBRUARY
MARCH
APRIL
MAY
JUNE
JULY
AUGUST
SEPTEMBER
OCTOBER
NOVEMBER
DECEMBER
phone: 615.298.3533 fax:2
e.mail: teamdesign@hom

I'm Ready to Move On

I'm tired to the bone and I want to be left alone
Let my memberships expire, read *Don Quixote* by the fire
Now there's a man apart, indeed, perched upon his stalwart steed
Fighting windmills with a stick and his friends all think he's sick

You know there'll come a day when none of this will matter
It will all be so much mindless chatter
And we won't look at each other and scoff
The day we turn the TV off

No right, no wrong, no weak, no strong
No black, no white, no dark, no light
No in, no out, no faith, no doubt
No red, no green, no fat, no lean
No hope, no fear, no week, no year
No rich, no poor, no less, no more
No round, no flat, no this, no that
No war, no hate, no church, no state
No prejudice, no edifice
No evidence, just common sense
No character fault, no pillar of salt
No point of attack, no knife in your back

I'm ready
I'm ready
I'm ready to move on

& THE OUTSIDERS

FEATURING

WILL KIMBROUGH

& JEDD HUGHES

NEW ALBUM

THE OUTSIDER

IN STORES

AUGUST 16th

Columbia Records, a division of SONY BMG Entertainment

"I'm the lapsed Buddhist son of a HELL-FIRE BREATHING, unknown TONGUE SPEAKING, Pentecostal mother. What else am I to do but strip search the HUMAN CONDITION for SIGNS of a song?"

TOUR2005

Michael Wilson

EPILOGUE

The first time I heard Rodney Crowell's recording of "Ain't No Money," I was left with the feeling that I needed to listen to everything he had ever written. He quickly became this eighteen-year-old college kid from Iowa's favorite artist, and somehow along the way we became friends. When I was asked by Rodney himself to help put his lyrical relevance into a few final words, it occurred to me that, as a singer and songwriter, he needs no help distilling his legacy into permanence. He was on the scene at the formation of the outlaw country movement, the late-eighties alt-country movement and, most notably, the birth of Americana music. He has grown from Guy Clark protégé and Hot Band taciturn rhythm guitarist and wunderkind songsmith into an elder statesman. It is impossible to fit every excellent song he has written into this, or any, anthology. The same goes for the compositions yet to come. However, as long as his songs play on radio stations, streaming services, home entertainment systems, and on the stages of live music venues around the world, he will remain the consummate philosopher, poet, and protector of all things pertaining to words and rhyme. And, no doubt, will be remembered as one of the greatest to ever do it. Plain as that.

— Michael Coady Sparks

+ AFTER all this time
I still Love you

These were Days
There were Times when we
so alive + Full of Hunger

Till
when TEAR DROPS fell on SA

I STILL W
I STILL Ne

I could never Let you
A BROKEN Heart that

you're ~~still~~ on my mind

ure always on my mind

were younger

ty kisses

t you

d you

id

als so slow

Many thanks to Ken Levitan, Scott B. Bomar, Karen Cronin, Lisa Jenkins, Dan Levitin, Gary Fisketjon, Ray Martin, Michael Coady Sparks, Hannah Sutherland, and Brian Ahern.

Love and abiding appreciation to Emmylou Harris, Rosanne Cash, Vince Gill, Will Jennings, Mary Karr, Donivan Cowart, Steuart Smith, Sterling Ball . . . and to those sweet souls in spirit form, J.W., Cauzette, Guy, Susanna, Larry (LeeRoy) Willoughby, Gary (US) Haber, Bo Goldsen, and Walter Martin Cowart.

The best of who I am and may yet become belongs to Claudia, my children, and their children.

Thomas Petillo